SLOW
DANCING
WITH
FIRE

SLOW
DANCING
WITH
FIRE

Photo: Georges Piette, 1980

a memoir of resilience

BRAHNA YASSKY

SHANTI ARTS PUBLISHING
BRUNSWICK, MAINE

Slow Dancing with Fire
a memoir of resilience

Published by Shanti Arts Publishing

Cover and interior design by Shanti Arts Designs

Cover image by Maxim Tajer at unsplash.com

Shanti Arts LLC
Brunswick, Maine
www.shantiarts.com

Printed in the United States of America

This book is a memoir, written from the author's recollections of
experiences that occurred over many years. The dialogue presented
in this book is not intended to represent word-for-word transcripts;
events and scenes are not precise representations. The names and
characteristics of some individuals have been changed to protect
privacy. In all cases, the author has remained true to the feeling and
meaning of what happened and what was said.

ISBN: 978-1-956056-27-3 (softcover)
ISBN: 978-1-956056-28-0 (ebook)

Library of Congress Control Number: 2022931971

To the memory of my parents,
Paula and Herbert Yassky,
and my brother, Jimmy Yassky.

You are always with me.

"What is to give light must endure burning."

—Viktor Frankl

CONTENTS

PROLOGUE

I STARTED WRITING THIS MEMOIR THIRTY YEARS AFTER literally being on fire. It took decades to approach conveying what happened in prose form. As a painter, I created random vignettes that indicated inevitable change but didn't portray the event, the scars, my vulnerability. I needed to hide behind my imagery, to feel the power as an artist who could visually reinterpret my world. I never wanted anyone to know the extent of the injuries or think of me as a burn victim. Yet, the ravage of the fire was a rehearsal for time's inevitable changes, which occur unexpectedly.

As I gained distance from that period in my life, I realized I was a survivor and had a story to tell about my transformation and the strength achieved through it. I internalized the ferocity of the flames that initially lit my skin. The power of the fire has been a slow burn fueling my energy, a driving force that propels me forward. Like most who have faced their own mortality and miraculously received more time, I have been determined to use it by living positively and productively.

❧

THE MEMOIR ENGAGES UNIVERSAL QUESTIONS ABOUT IDENTITY, beauty and the struggle between wanting to be seen and wanting to be invisible. Obsessed with celebrity kids, as a child, I wanted people to notice me. I was not a pre-pubescent sex kitten like Annette Funicello on The Mickey Mouse Club or cute and outgoing like Patty Duke. I was skinny hunching my shoulders and never looking anyone in the face as not to blind them with the glare of my braces and glasses, more comfortable writing about who I wanted to be.

At nine, on a toy typewriter, I hammered out all my sisterly virtues, which I had to make up, since in reality my six-year old brother Jimmy and I always fought. I truly believed he saw me as mean, ugly, and horrible. This entry, to which I signed his name, set forth the reasons he wanted to win presents for me on the *Little Big Payoff*, a quiz show whose hostess, Bess Myerson, the first Jewish Miss America, was an inspiration in our community.

They chose the letter and we felt instantly famous. My mother bought me a dress with short white puffy sleeves, navy bodice and flared skirt covered with tiny raised white Swiss polka dots that looked like nonpareils. I wore neatly cuffed white socks and black Mary Janes. She set my perfect short haircut parted on the side the night before and styled it with pomade gel like Natalie Wood's in "Rebel Without a Cause." Jimmy wore a gray suit, button down white shirt and tie, making him look like a miniature man.

Sitting on the red cushioned throne, without my glasses I embodied my ideal, skirt spread like a canopy over my legs, ankles crossed. "What's your favorite food?" the only question the host Bob Paige asked me. "Baked clams." He chuckled and the audience did too. He then turned to Jimmy holding three white cards in his hand. "OK young man are you ready win your lovely sister some prizes?" Jimmy nodded. "What material did the three little pigs use so the wolf couldn't blow their house down?"

"Brick," Jimmy said without hesitation

"Correct. Looks like we may have a future architect here. You have just won your sister a gold plated necklace and a Betty Cocker Jr. cookbook." I smiled close –mouthed.

"Next, for two Schwinn bikes, who is the president of the United States?"

"Dwight D. Eisenhower" Jimmy replied his skinny chest puffing up his shirt.

"Correct again. Now for the final question and a chance to win this beagle puppy." Bess Myerson walked on stage holding the cutest puppy with big, soft floppy ears. My eyes fixed on the living bundle, I muttered under my breath please-get-it-right, please-get-it-right. "What is the capital of New York State?" he asked.

Jimmy stood so erect he appeared to grow a few inches, paused and after what seemed to be ten minutes, he answered. "Albany."

The audience cheered. Bess Myerson handed me the puppy. I was thrilled to share the same stage with her and be the focus of an audience of thousands. She ushered us off the stage. A photographer took our picture in front of glamorous gold brocade drapery.

Feeling invisible as an artist after the fire and once again able to use my burned arm, I made a 6' x 4' painting of that day. I painted Bess Meyerson, Bob Paige, Jimmy and me standing in front of the gorgeous brocade curtain inside a television set. I realized Bess and I had identical hairdos. Making the painting and reliving the day helped me to remember that I wasn't really invisible.

Yet, sometimes I wanted to be. On a steamy summer day, I wore Jobst scar compression garments all over my body and a loose cotton skirt, blouse, and hat to cover the Jobst. I couldn't tolerate the heat while waiting outside a restaurant for a friend; my first trip to a cafe alone since the fire. Around me, people wore tees and shorts. I opened the door, delighting in the cold blast of air conditioning. Sitting in a cushioned booth, the waiter approached. I ordered a strawberry daiquiri.

"Can you pay for it?" he asked.

"Why would I order something I couldn't pay for?" I said

"You look like a homeless person, wearing all those clothes," he answered. I ran out in tears and didn't go to a restaurant again for months unless buffered by friends or relatives.

∽

WHEN I ARRIVED AT AN ARTIST RESIDENCY IN BALI IN FEBRUARY 2019, nestled in my room, I listened to a torrential rainstorm swish through the lush vegetation. I felt disoriented and jet-lagged from thirty hours of travel, yet comforted. Water had that effect on me. My project evolved into an installation of writing, drawing and water ritual, the elements that have healed me since 1982.

The act of writing this book has reawakened the strength I summoned to build a new life, decades ago.

1

HEAT

IT SLIPPED OUT OF A BOOK. THE BLACK-AND-WHITE photograph's scalloped white edges indicated it had to be at least ten years old. I ran my finger over the perimeter, hesitating to turn it over not knowing what memory would jump out at me. I saw my twenty-year-old self in a bikini with patterned scarf tied around my head gypsy-style. The glaring sun above made me appear as a shadow, my stance confident—thin, doe legs forming a V firmly rooted in the sand, hands on my hips. That was the summer of 1970. I had spent a month living outdoors in a secluded cove on a beach in Mykonos with Kevin, the first man I almost married. I had loved the way the heat had penetrated my skin all day and burned it to a shade so much darker than the one I was born with.

∽

TWELVE YEARS LATER, I SLIP INTO MY PAINTING CLOTHES—BLACK paint-splattered jeans and soft pink top—focusing on how to begin my new painting.

I fill a blue kettle with water, place it on a burner of the stove, automatically turning on the flame and putting a paper filter into the coffee maker; then cut a green kiwi and ripe strawberries oozing their red juice. The trucks rumble on the cobblestone street and the soft, cool light outside the window suffuses my loft. At the sound of gurgling, I distractedly remove the kettle from the burner's waving cobalt blue flame to pour the water over the coffee.

Suddenly my arm feels warm, then hot. I smell something burning, a mixture of barbecue and melting plastic. The pungent smell is close. Very close. I look for the source. It is me! Orange flames dangle from the wide sleeve of my polyester, pink chenille sweater. For a moment, I stare at my arm in disbelief as if it were a separate entity. Yet I feel the extreme heat. I am on fire! I AM ON FIRE. I AM ON FIRE. My mind shouts and wonders, *should I roll on the floor? Then what if the wood floor catches on fire?* I'm here alone. I quickly gasp for air through my mouth, hyperventilating. Then can't breathe. So scared, I can't move. My brain freezes. Hot ice. Time stops. A statue, I watch the flame for a second. A spark bounces through the air and lands on the cuff at my ankle. My arm stings as if attacked by thousands of bees. The piercing pain spreads, every nerve buzzing, my brain reconnects. Trembling, I dash to my front door and run through the hallway screaming for help. In motion, I hear the sizzle of my flesh and clothes, smell my singed hair and smoked skin. The flames spread. Their glow lights the dark landing.

My neighbor Tony rushes down the stairs. He rapidly rips off my clothes and swats me with a rough blanket. Large pieces of cloth glue to my body as if holding me together. Vibrating with my own shrill cries, the screams combine with the whirling of sirens. It's a flash in time. It's forever. Fast thumping footsteps, voices, equipment hitting the walls. Men are carrying me suspended and bumping down the stairs. The cold air blows across my face, and out of the edge of an eye, I see the red of fire engines. A small crowd of people gathers on the street as the EMS lift and load me onto a stretcher into the darkness of an ambulance speeding to St. Vincent's Hospital in Greenwich Village.

※

I OPEN MY EYES TO A PRIEST HOVERING OVER ME, MAKING THE SIGN of the cross. He is giving me last rites. This can't be, I think. I'm Jewish.

Then all I see is a white light. I feel it slightly tugging my feet toward the calmness of vanishing. It would be comfortable and very easy to surrender and slip into that void. Yet my head fills with images that thwart the gentle slide out of my body. In a blurry bubble, I see large vague paintings I haven't created yet. Jake, the second man I almost married, stands smiling while holding the hand of an unfamiliar small blond child. Jake is a fisherman in California I left years before. Who is this child?

A voice crashes in my head. You're on fire, you're hot, you're unstoppable, blazing forward, a force no one can touch. I incorporate the power that could destroy me. I decide to fight for my life, focusing on a glowing glimpse of a future.

The flash of an overly bright light sears through the darkness behind my closed eyelids. I strain to open my eyes and see a man in a white coat with a surgical mask over his nose and mouth holding a camera. He pulls down the sheet with one hand, exposing my charred body. I feel the air brush my skin like an attack of jellyfish. I hear the continual click of the camera and see him snapping pictures of my torso, leg, arm, and neck. My body quivers with the effort to scream "NO." I am not a specimen. I am determined to live, and with that resolve, although I cannot move, I want to cover myself with a shredding shawl of vanity to prevent documentation of my devastated body.

I hear floating random phrases: "55% damage, lucky she's alive"; "arm burned beyond repair, amputate"; "her mother says she's a painter"—*Where is my mother?* I wonder—"only thirty, won't have the will to live without her arm"—*Is my arm really that damaged?* I think, dizzy with panic—"I can sew it on".

I open my eyes and see a woman in her early forties, a decade older than me, in a white coat with blond hair, a gentle smile on her beautiful, yet serious face. She stares at my eyes, making sure I register what she is telling me. "I'm Dr. Haher. I will save your arm," she says. Buoyed, I will float and not drown. I take a breath that fills my sore belly. I know that as long as I am in her care I will be safe. Then I pass out.

∽

LAYING ON A BED NEAR A WINDOW, THE NORTHERN EXPOSURE CASTS a soft consistent light on my corner of the room in the burn unit. White hanging curtains cloister the bed from the five others of which I am not yet aware. Confused, I think I am in my bed at home where white parachutes, the inspiration for my first painting series, billow on the walls and ceiling. However, this white material is stiffer, more opaque. What I hear is the drip, drip, dripping, beep, beep, beeping and bubbling from the machines attached to my arms and throat. I can't move. I look down to see a gauze-covered cocoon encase my body. Blood and puss ooze through the layers of wrapped bandages. Guardrails enclose my bed like a giant crib. My mother is sitting next to the bed. The furrows on her forehead deepen as she studies me. Her large dark eyes behind her glasses are swimming in tears. This scares me even more. When she notices I'm awake, she strokes my cheek and forces a smile.

"I'm hot. I can't stand the burning pain," I gasp. She gently places a cool washcloth on my forehead. I will feel this act of comfort for the rest of my life. Her hand and body leaning over me makes me feel less alone in my intense pain and desperation. "Mommy, please don't leave," I cry as the nurse she has summoned increases the morphine drip, and I become numb. I hear her voice, which sounds far away, answer, "I won't."

I travel from the hospital bed with the gurgling machines that will save my life into the past of being twenty-five, pretty, and in love on Jake's fishing boat; the salty wind moistening my face and whipping back my long hair flying like a mast.

I can hardly breathe when the lurking fear of not knowing how my life will be takes over my mind. My breath is fast and shallow, my chest not moving below my throat. In that moment I instinctively know that the only way I can get through this is to make art of the horror, to make a film of this day, recreating it as the director, not the protagonist. With that consoling thought, I drift off.

∾

MY BODY TWITCHES WHEN I HEAR THE CRIES, SHOUTS, AND MOANS from the patients in the other beds. Their pain amplifies my own. The hushed conversations of the hospital staff, the beeping, humming, ringing, and gurgling of all the machines in the room make me anxious, and I can't sleep except when I am drugged. The worst time to be awake is 4 a.m.

∾

JUST A FEW MONTHS BEFORE, 4 A.M. WAS THE TIME I RETURNED home from the Mudd Club, the notorious dive on White Street filled with black lights, loud music, boys who looked like girls, girls who looked like boys, and everyone else who looked fabulous. With my smooth skin as a fashion accessory, I applied heavy eyeliner and shadow to my bedroom-eyes, wore my shortest, tightest black clothes. The bouncer whisked me right past the velvet red ropes that formed a barricade to the crowds on the sidewalk. He knew me. I belonged. Jean Michel Basquiat, Blondie, Adam Ant, Lou Reed, Klaus Nomi performed and hung out.

I entered the cave of gyrating bodies where any desire to obliterate the outside world could be satisfied—drugs, sex, small talk, big talk, new connections—luxuriating in bathing in the darkness of the downtown urban nightlife. I danced wildly for hours with always available guys. A smoke cloud of seductive danger lurked in every slow dance wrapped in the arms of a stranger in the dim lit club a few blocks from my loft. The DJ spinning James Brown's "I Feel Good" sent me out on the floor, thrusting my hips, shimmying my shoulders.

When my brother, Jimmy, and his boyfriend, Jacques, were there, they pulled me into the cluster they formed with other beautiful boys in a blissful tug of communal movement. Afterward we went to Dave's Luncheonette on Canal Street, joining a group of people for a post Mudd Club egg cream, my favorite childhood drink. The belligerent waitress who had to work through the night serving party goers made the perfect combination of chocolate syrup, milk, and seltzer to counteract or enhance drug or alcohol highs. She served the glasses by sliding them down the counter, not wanting to get too close to the customers.

I never saw my favorite dance partner, Bobby, at Dave's or anywhere outside the dark club. He looked like a throwback to the fifties and moved like Elvis. He combed his jet black hair into a towering stiff duckbill, wore pointy black shoes, tight black pants, and black sports jacket with sequined musical notes on the lapel.

Rushing down Lispenard Street one day toward the back entrance of Pearl Paint, thinking about the colors I needed to paint my canvas of a four-foot bicep, a thin figure weaving down the street interrupted my motion. I looked at his face. "Hey, Bobby," I said, somewhat taken aback. He gave me a flaccid hug. His clothes felt stiff with dried sweat. "How ya doin'?" he said, smiling, exposing his jagged tobacco-stained teeth. The smeared eyeliner accentuated his vacant eyes. I noticed his acne scarred, sickly pale skin for the first time. That daylight glimpse of the nightlife made me feel woozy and nauseous like a contact hangover. I rushed into the art store and headed for the second floor, wandering through the aisles of art supplies that contained the raw materials of my life. Tubes and cans of oils lined up according to brands. Perusing the colors, I selected the ones I wanted, put them into my red plastic shopping basket, and hurried back to my studio.

∽

I OPEN MY EYES THE NEXT MORNING IN THE BURN UNIT AND MY mother slips a little machine that makes the sounds of the ocean under my pillow to block out the unwanted noise and to calm me. She hands me a magic slate because the tube in my throat makes it difficult to talk. I write messages that are erased after they are read, leaving nothing but the blank gray plastic slate.

The only other patient I actually see is a little girl in the bed next to me. I hear a nurse say that someone dunked her in scalding water. I gasp when I see her small red body brought in and gently placed on a bed. For the first time I feel sorrier for someone other than myself. Since then the drapes between our beds have been drawn. I hear her continual whimpering.

One day the sound stops. The staff removes the machines on the other side of the curtain, and her mother's cries grow fainter as the sound of her heavy footsteps becomes silent. The little girl dies. I ring for the nurse to bring the bedpan and I vomit. I have the first tangible proof that very few patients leave by walking out of the burn unit.

ᔕ

I MEASURE TIME BY BEING AWAKE—HOSPITAL TIME—OR SEDATED— when my mind goes back to the parts of my life that feel safe or exciting. The morphine creates a hazy barrier from the pain. Airborne like a fly, I hover above my body, flitting back and forth between past and present, blending disjointed time and events.

In my head, I map out scene by scene, a film recreating the few minutes in the day that changed my world. Although I don't want to be the character in my own film, oddly, a memory appears of my first identification with a character in a movie and my desire for that life to be mine. I was sixteen. Alone on the subway, my legs stuck to the course tan woven seats in the summer heat of 1965. I lived for those biweekly rides that took me to Greenwich Village from Manhattan Beach in Brooklyn. At the Bleecker Street Cinema, I lost myself in the films of Godard and Antonioni. Images flickered in black and white, sometimes color. The heroine, just a few years older than I was, had a life that seemed so much more real and alive. I wanted that exciting drama. Departing the small theater, I was Jean Seberg in *Breathless*, Catherine Deneuve in *Umbrellas of Cherbourg,* or whatever gamin whose world I had slipped into for two hours. I clung to that identity, sipping coffee at the Café Figaro down the block.

ᔕ

WHEN THE NURSE APPROACHES MY BED TO INCREASE THE MORPHINE level, I know I am about to be wheeled to a special room for debriding. After a soak in an antiseptic tub, the nurse places me on a sterilized metal table under bright lights while her tiny scissors and tweezers, like a bird's beak, prick, pick, and snip away the scarlet burned skin, like raw meat, cutting it from sections of my body. The fire had moved on a sloppy diagonal path, starting from my right arm across the front and back of my torso and neck to my left leg. I howl. "Not too many people live through being burned like this," the nurse says. "This is the worst pain you will ever have to endure and you will recover. Something happens to everyone."

All I can feel is stinging pain like being in the middle of a wasp nest. A switch in my mind clicks to distracting thoughts to remove me from the present. As I watch the snipping, my mind sees the contrast of my body to the flawless exposed torso and white breasts of a woman riding a horse in *Equestrienne*, a painting by Chagall, and I drift off.

∽

MR. NELSON, MY FIRST COLLEGE ART TEACHER, HAD INSTRUCTED us to make a painting replicating a great work of art. I chose the Chagall, using watercolors. "Your strokes show you're not that comfortable with the medium yet. It's a little stiff, but well done," he said. "You can be a good painter one day. But first you need to make more paintings." I was convinced.

∽

I OPEN MY EYES. "YOU'LL BE OK," THE NURSE SAYS. "BE THANKFUL your face wasn't burned." The only certainty I have is that my life will never be the same as it had been. I am very different from the young woman in my first self-portrait painted just six years earlier in California in 1976. In the painting, I sit cross-legged on a red folded sleeping bag on the sidewalk, wearing white drawstring pants rolled up mid-calf and white leather roller skates. My naked torso, exposing my small breasts, is leaning forward toward the viewer— an act of freedom to convince myself their attraction lay in attitude not size. My long dark hair falls past my shoulders. I wear a big smile and white cat eye sunglasses with white ice skates glued to the bridge and tiny plastic couples in formal dress waltzing toward my temples. The painting summed up my life—part child, part woman gliding through experiences, attending art school in Oakland, and enamored with my lover Billy who created the props I used for my self-portrait. He defined my world—a local celebrity artist and curator of an art space in the town of Mill Valley where we both lived but not together. From twenty-six to thirty, my connection to him made me feel unfettered by the future and free to explore myself as an artist. I studied painting with photo realist teachers at school and learned about surrealism, Dada, and alternative rock music of Brian Eno, David Bowie, Devo, and Brian Ferry from Mickey aka Justin Otherear. Whether I was in his studio or he in mine, I tingled just seeing him. His penis bulged in his baggy white pants and he sighed. "We both have so much work to do but . . . " When alone in my studio, I lazily slid my hand down my panties while reading a book about Man Ray, merging Mill Valley with Paris of the thirties, imagining Billy and me as Man Ray and Lee Miller in the midst of the surrealist movement in an orgasmic fantasy.

I took photographs of anything in my life that was symbolic or reflective of what I thought, felt, or saw. Reinterpreting the images into paintings kept me absorbed in my studio for hours. I made a large oil painting of Billy inside a phone booth, his forearm and hand pressing the numbers on the dial, the other hand holding the receiver, his face reflected on the shiny metal surface behind the buttons. Who knew the painting would document a relic of communication no longer commonly available or even recognizable to following generations? I was learning my skill using an emotionally connected content for my work. My teachers encouraged my subject matter, which differed from most of the leading photo realists of the seventies, the vast majority men, with the exception of Audrey Flack. They used images of American culture like diners, cars, suburban houses, city architecture, or signage.

∽

BACK IN MY BED, THE YOUNG RESIDENT WITH A BOW TIE HOVERS over my bared nakedness. He scrutinizes the freshly exposed areas and orders Betadine. He then wraps my wounds as if I was a fragile package. I call for a nurse to help with my pain. Before she comes, to get my mind off my stinging skin, I wonder if this young adorable doctor would have been attracted to me when I worked my way through art school as an artist model.

I think about that other me who worked as a cocktail waitress in a disco in Sausalito. Perched on a hill, the bar's panoramic windows overlooked the water with the distant light of houses and boats below. Inside the disco music pumped, the patrons echoed "uh, uh, uh, uh" to *Staying Alive* by the Bee Gees. Wearing a tight turquoise-and black-striped cap sleeve tee shirt, my long hair pulled to the side in a perky ponytail, I smoothly glided between them. I carried a little round tray above my head dwarfed by the professional athletes who occasionally tipped me $20 for bringing them their

Courvoisier. Those well-toned titans inspired a series of paintings of muscular male body parts juxtaposed to the Nautilus machines that augmented them. Years later, as an awakened feminist, I would realize that I was using the female gaze to reverse the centuries-old tradition by painting the idealized male body from a woman's point of view as a metaphor. None of the figures had heads.

"Feeling down again?" the nurse says, holding the needle and drip bag. "But you're so popular. Every day, this really cute guy comes to see you."

"He's my brother."

∽

I close my eyes and remember visiting Jimmy in 1978 in New York. In that last year at art school with a few exhibits under my belt, including my self-portrait in a group show, I started dreaming of New York. Something extraordinary was hatching there, the city was dangling promises of fame, and I wanted to be a part of it. I went back for a visit.

"It's Halloween and we need outrageous costumes so we can get into Studio 54," Jimmy said. "We" included his law partner Neal and Jacques. "You're the artist, any ideas?" he asked me. Inspired by the recent first successful test tube baby, I suggested we go as a new kind of family. I dressed Jimmy in a polka dot shirt, sports jacket, polka dot baseball cap, and sunglasses as the dad. Jacques, as mom, wore a tight knee-length dress stuffed with onions as breasts, and a rainbow afro. I carefully applied his makeup. Towering inches above six feet, Neal found heels, a nurse's dress and cap, and wore a Groucho Marx mask. I was the baby in a transparent plastic jacket that reached mid-thigh, white baby bib, cloth diaper, and a rubber-nipple pacifier around my neck. As a moving ensemble, not only did we waltz into Studio 54, but Andy Warhol followed us around and took our picture. We danced through the night. A naked man and woman rode through the club on a white horse. Bianca Jagger held court.

I visited Soho galleries during the day, the streets lined with exhibition spaces and potential. When I returned to California, I made plans to move. I was going home.

∽

I feel movement next to my bed and hear Jimmy call my name. He takes my hand. "I was just thinking about when you came back to New York and lived with Jacques and me before you got your loft," he says. Although I'm woozy, the memory of my first few months in Tribeca is vivid. I took a Christmas seasonal job in Bloomingdale's selling men's shirts on the ground floor. In the frenzy of shoppers, every now and then among the thousands of credit cards handed to me, I saw a name like Henry Kissinger or Al Pacino. Having handed back the card after the name registered in my head, I saw the ghost of celebrity vanish in the crowd. I dwelled in the fantasy of being on the other side of the counter being the one looked at in awe, even though I knew that only a small percent of artists became famous, and their faces were not their currency of recognition.

I look at Jimmy and remember him saying, "It's unbelievable. You've only been here two months from mellow Marin and already scored a great loft and a gallery uptown to show your work. By next week you'll meet your husband."

"Not a chance," I laughed, lighting an unfiltered Camel with his. "I'm married to my art." We sat at the orange kitchen counter in his loft. Jacques was preparing dinner. "Let me do something." I volunteered taking the placemats, flatware, and plates to the table across the room.

"Merci," Jacques said. Thanks to them, I had a coterie of beautiful, fun, gay friends. Little did we know that in fifteen years they would all be gone.

∽

AS WEEKS WENT BY IN THE HOSPITAL, I STARTED GETTING MAIL. I received a postcard of van Gogh's *Starry Nights*. Written on the back in a flourishing hand, it said, "Dear Brahna, Best wishes for a speedy recovery. I hope you get to go outside soon and look at the stars. When you do, paint them for me. Love, Vincent."

This anonymous pen pal who knew what I liked and gave me hope fascinated me. Who was it? When my parents and brother denied authorship, I begged them to find out. I needed to know who cared that much about me returning to my art.

∽

BACK IN MY MORPHINE DREAM, I SAW MY STUDIO IN MILL VALLEY, California. I'd completed my first series of paintings there—my parachute paintings. I shared the ground floor with a roommate. The big room, which had been the sanctuary, with its high ceiling and gigantic front wall of leaded pane glass windows, facing the leafy trees, was my studio and bedroom. Hanging white parachutes cordoned off a corner of the room housing my bed, a foam mattress atop a handcrafted wood platform on legs and a flea market antique dresser.

I immersed myself in a constructed world of large segments of parachutes, working late into the night. In the silence of the small town nestled in the trees, I felt as if I were the only person awake. The process of painting was a comforting blanket. I loved the physicality of putting together the wooden stretcher bars of five or six feet, making sure all corners were at the same angle by measuring the diagonals, tapping here and there to create the perfect square or rectangle. I pulled the canvas across the frame so tightly it sounded like a drum when I tapped the somewhat daunting white expanse awaiting me. I slowly rolled my spine up from bending forward, stacking each vertebra on top of the other. My world was in order ready to proceed. Creating the parachute paintings, I learned how to connect emotions and abstract thoughts through a visual continuity that I couldn't verbalize. I found a language through color, composition, and the metaphor of parachutes blurring and obscuring what lay behind them. I applied the buttery white and pale oils hyper-realistically, depicting parts of the sensual creases and texture billowing in different patterns, hinting at someone behind them. While I was painting I felt at home in myself.

In the process of painting the exaggerated folds, I usually thought of sex with Billy—his waist-length blond hair, perfect round butt. In addition to thinking he was hot, what drew me to him was his creative genius and lack of caring about status, money, or ambition.

Although we lived several blocks from each other, we spent parts of most nights and days together for four years. I didn't understand why he would never refer to me as his girlfriend or us as a couple. On an afternoon visit, not seeing him in his studio, I assumed he was taking a nap on the foam-covered floor in his adjoining bedroom. Anticipating a spontaneous afternoon tryst, I climbed across the foam, which felt unusually lumpy.

As I approached, leaning into him to snuggle, he said, "You have to leave."

"Why? You look like you're waiting for me."

"Someone else is here," he whispered.

In disbelief, I tried to pull down the covers and said, "Who?"

He took my hand and said in a firm but soft voice. "Just go." I turned quickly so he wouldn't see me crying and stomped over the body under the quilt, slammed the door, smashing a row of Pez dispensers on a shelf along the way, and ran back to my studio. I would never trust him, and although still obsessed with him, I'd let that feeling run its course. I knew I wouldn't give a man that power again. Yet I couldn't stop seeing him. I transferred my mixture of insecurity, desire, longing, and betrayal to painting the intricate folds of the parachutes. The pleasure of mixing the tactile paints into the consistency of cake frosting was foreplay before applying them to my complexly shrouded world on the canvas. In my studio, using my whole body, I could bury my musings, mesmerized by the challenge of creating the illusion of the silky texture.

༄

NOW, WRAPPED IN SOFT GAUZE, IMMOBILE, TUCKED UNDER TIGHT white sheets, I was as trapped as I had been free.

For the first two months in the burn unit, I only wanted my family to visit me. I didn't want any of my friends seeing me dazed, confined, and damaged.

If anything was a pleasure, food came close. The click of high heels on the linoleum floor and the smell of tea rose perfume battling the antiseptic odors signaled the arrival of Aunt Sylvia bringing goodies from Balducci's. My favorite aunt, Sylvia, a wealthy psychiatrist's widow in her sixties, decked out in her diamonds, Elizabeth Taylor-style black wig, Cleopatra eye makeup and designer clothes, actually resembled the movie star with whom she shared a hairdo. Adding to her happy nature, she delighted in buying things, and since that's how she spent most of her time, she had one of those mouths fixed in a smile. She plopped herself down on the chair next to me, squeezed my hand, and blew air kisses. Then she took out our feast from the oversized shopping bag item by item, filling my tray table. She piled some shrimp on a plate, holding it close to my mouth while I clumsily held the fork and speared them.

Although the food was delicious, feeding myself was exhausting and moving my arm painful. On her way out my aunt sent the nurse in.

2

WATER'S EDGE

D RIFTING IN A MORPHINE HAZE, THE TOUCH OF MY mother's soft hand stroking my face transforms me back to being a small child on the sand at Brooklyn's Manhattan Beach, which was sparsely dotted with residents and the occasional clam or mussel shell.

My mother brushed the sand out of my eyes when the kids ran by as I rested on our blanket after spending hours making an alternative world of intricate sand castles. She and her friend Eileen sat close in their aluminum and woven plastic beach chairs creating our own little encampment. The sand was soft but close enough to the water for an unimpaired view. Jimmy and his friend Charlie, Eileen's son, took turns attempting to bury each other in the sand then toddled toward the ocean. Eileen jumped up, breasts jiggling in her low-cut, Marilyn Monroe-inspired, polka dot bathing suit, heavily made up Betty Boop eyes attentively wide. My mother looked less flashy, trim, and fashionable in her leopard-print bathing suit. Even at the beach, she wore her black hair in an impeccably neat and natural bob, sunglasses masking her unmade-up eyes. Persian melon—a popular pinkish orange—lipstick and nail polish flawlessly covered her mouth, fingers, and toenails.

I open my eyes in the hospital to see that same hair and lipstick twenty-five years later. Comforted, I close them again.

❧

MANHATTAN BEACH WAS THE ONLY SHORELINE COMMUNITY IN Brooklyn that didn't have a boardwalk or food concessions. Residents simply walked down the block to the ocean. The knish man, clad in white shirt and baggy khaki pants, trudged across the hot sand in heavy black shoes with bulging brown paper shopping bags in each hand. The bags contained large patties of baked dough filled with coarsely mashed potatoes, each one individually wrapped in wax paper—a popular snack for the resident descendants of European Jews.

"Hot knishes," he shouted. My mother waved her hand and he appeared, casting a shadow over her asking, "How many? Do you want salt?"

I loved the comforting taste and texture of the hot potato filling as it slid down my throat. After Jimmy and I ate our knishes and packed lunches of hard-boiled eggs and carrot sticks, we looked forward to our dessert. In the haze of the heat, kicking up sand, appearing like the Lone Ranger without a mask, the ice cream man approached. He was dressed all in white with a hard black box attached to a black diagonal strap across the front of his shirt. A white plastic helmet hid most of the beads of sweat on his forehead. The vanilla ice cream on a stick covered in crispy chocolate coating was my favorite and would continue to be for decades.

∾

MY LIPS ARE COOL AND MOIST. A NURSE STANDING NEXT TO MY BED is brushing them with an ice cube from a cup. She pops in a cube when I open my mouth. My throat is dry as sand. My mother, sitting next to my bed, smiles politely at her and takes the cup in case I want more. Her brow is furrowed. She looks tired. She has been sitting there for hours. When she notices I'm awake she smiles. She sighs and says, "We'll get through this together. I will stay for as long as you want me to."

∾

DRIFTING IN AND OUT, I PICTURE HER SIPPING HER MORNING coffee at the breakfast room table, the *New York Times* obituary section opened in front of her. I never knew why she read it. She didn't comment on it. But, observing her daily ritual from an early age, I reasoned that only if there was an article written about you when you died was your life worth living. In my head, it set the tone for one of the purposes of my life: to be famous or at least sufficiently well known for the world to notice or care when I was no longer there. I wanted that but how was I going to do it when I felt invisible? When I was young, people noticed girls for being pretty, and I never received that kind of admiration. How would I make my mark? Eleanor Roosevelt was one of a few female role models, but along with Marilyn Monroe and Elizabeth Taylor, the ideals of beauty and womanhood, I could never live up to them.

When I was a teenager, my father said, 'Be grateful you're not beautiful. When a man falls in love with you it will be because of who you are." My grandmother told me she heard some kids saying I looked like a bag of bones. "Eat, Bubbala, you'll look better," was her advice. I didn't realize then that her attitude reflected having fled the pogroms in Russia alone when barely a teenager and starting her American life in poverty on the Lower East Side. Having more than enough to eat was an achievement to enjoy and was reflected in pinchable, round cheeks.

In my mind, the way I wanted to stand out in my high school of 5,000 students, a microcosm of competitive high-achieving grownups in New York City, was to be a cheerleader. Shy by nature, but having danced with my mother to *American Bandstand* in our basement for years, I knew how to move. We twisted to Chubby Checker, did the Lindy together, mimicking the steps of the cool Philly regulars like Carmen and Joey, mom throwing in some of her jitterbug arm waving, and did the mashed potato, heels clicking, sliding on the linoleum floor. I practiced the cheers as diligently as studying for my honor classes. After each series of tryouts, the tension mounted. When Mrs. Shapiro, the judge, finally chose me, I shrieked with joy and relief.

It didn't take long to realize that it was not the claim to fame I was looking for, but rather a commitment to show up for football games Saturday mornings, even if it was really cold, and basketball games Friday nights, even if I was tired. I actually had no interest in these sports.

However, I liked rocking my hips forward and back while moving my arms rhythmically through our routine, screaming L-I-N-C-O-L-N. I took my cue from the others when to jump up and down because we scored, not knowing the rules of the game, but nonetheless feeling I belonged.

And now look at me, the part of my brain that remembers I'm burned buzzes. I knew I would never again look like the young woman I became who didn't have to do anything except show up to be noticed. It would be months after the fire before I would dare to look in a mirror. I didn't know what I looked like but knew the damage was extensive. If I made it through, it would involve an interior excavation uncovering a part of me I valued beneath the surface.

As she leans over the rails of the hospital bed to smooth my hair, I think about how my mother has always been there even when I thought I didn't want her to be. Before leaving for college, she inserted herself in every part of my life. In the same basement where we danced together, she insisted on joining my teenage parties. She kept track of everything I did, everyone I knew. I hated that, yet on the other hand, she gently repeated that she was my confidante, and I told her all my dreams and fears. When I went to California to avoid having a life that remotely resembled hers, she sent me missives of love and encouragement. She wanted me to be educated and adventurous, to live the way she might have if she hadn't married at nineteen. Of course, it was a different time, and I was not her, so I never led her imagined alternate fantasy. She never had to create herself in the world, living under the protective identity of wife and mother. It was fun being an artist, being free from the compromise of a relationship, but there was no one to shield me. I made my own armor and enticing web with my art.

"Ma, remember when I showed a couple of my parachute paintings at a gallery at the San Francisco Museum of Modern Art about a year out of art school? I wore a one-piece parachute outfit at the opening. I wanted to blend with my work."

"How could I forget? I flew out from New York for the occasion. I still remember the first thing I said when I saw you: 'This is not my shy little girl anymore. You and your paintings look wonderful.' And I meant it."

"And I was so flattered but embarrassed by the extravagance of your trip. I told my friends you had to be in San Francisco anyway."

"I pretended that was true and didn't say anything different."

↬

THE BLOND DOCTOR WHO LOOKS LIKE A MOVIE STAR APPROACHES MY BED in a white jacket and bow tie. I feel dread because I know the drill. He unravels the gauze, exposing my raw flesh to the air. On these occasions, I catch glimpses of my burned skin in sections, which looks like freshly ground chopped meat. Sometimes, it's the skin held together with staples on the carnage on my ankle and lower leg; other times it's my right arm or stomach. They pump up my morphine to reduce my agony. Before the wave of dullness takes effect, I feel humiliation coupled with pain. This gorgeous young doctor is examining my grotesqueness. Would someone as handsome as he or any man ever find me desirable again? I long for the time my body was my tool of attraction. Those days are gone, but I want to remember them. I drift off, numbed by morphine and am back in Sausalito.

∽

IT's 1973. THE FIRST TIME I SAW JAKE ON HIS WOODEN FISHING boat. Bare-chested, he looked like a page in my anatomy art book that had lines pointing to and labeling each muscle. I had met and danced with him the night before at a party on a houseboat and assumed he was some kind of artist like everyone else there.

"You don't look like the pot-bellied smelly fishermen I see unloading their catch on the dock," I said. "Two months ago I was a computer programmer," he answered. This was even more surprising to me.

I'd never touched a computer nor known anyone else who had. "But what are you doing on this boat?" I asked.

"Since I was a kid I always wanted to be a fisherman. When my aunt died, she left me a wad of dough. I decided to go for it and bought myself this sweet little boat, *The Gale*."

That's interesting, I thought. I had taken a break from my studio to walk along the Sausalito docks but needed to get back to drawing. I started sketching Jake after seeing him with his shirt off. I returned the next morning with muffins and coffee, wearing my little white sundress patterned with blue flowers.

After eating on the deck, he showed me the rest of the boat. We climbed down a ladder where there was a wooden table collapsed on its hinges. Built-in wood benches and cabinets lined the sides. The hull was a mattress over drawers with a porthole toward its point.

"How cozy," I said.

"Come here," he beckoned as he climbed on the bed. I shook my head no.

"You don't waste any time."

"You came back, didn't you?"

I smiled, tilting my head to the side as I pulled a little of my hair across my cheek twirling it. He was moving too fast for me; I never slept with someone before getting to know him. I stepped back and turned to climb the stairs. I felt his eyes follow me. I ascended each step slowly not quite sure if I really wanted to leave. I turned and he was on the edge of the bed, head cocked in an awkward position trying to look up my skirt, his expression a mixture of sweetness and desire. I continued up the stairs laughing to myself. I was getting turned on by his intense attention. Once on the deck I heard a bang. He bounded up the stairs, bumping his head while leaping to the deck.

"I'm sorry if I misread the clues. Just got divorced and am sort of out of practice. I really dig you. Please stay."

Sitting on the deck, I asked him about his marriage. He told me his ex-wife looked like Ann-Margaret and had betrayed him. His mother was a university art professor and potter. He did not look devious or sleazy in any way as he bent down to kiss me and then carried me down the stairs. Jake had an Olympic swimmer's body. Despite his six feet, four inches to my five feet, four inches, we fit together like a puzzle.

As we lay in a post-coital daze, Jake said, "Let's grab some lunch. I heard the Trident's pretty good."

After lunch he said he needed to get some parts for the boat and invited me to have dinner later. I was satiated but knew that by evening my hunger would return and agreed to meet him at *The Gale.* That evening I packed a large purse with my contact lens case and solution, a change of clothes, and makeup. When I arrived, flower petals carpeted the boat deck. Jake, dressed in a clean but wrinkled button-down shirt and jeans, handed me a gardenia for my hair.

"The engine works well enough for a putter. How about Tiburon for dinner?"

We docked the funky fishing boat among the yachts at a fancy waterside restaurant. Unlike me, Jake felt quite at home with conservative California wealth. Loping alongside of me, one arm was around my waist, the other swung freely as we followed the hostess to our seats. His laugh, a goofy giggle, was the only distinct sound in the hushed room.

For the next two weeks, except for several hours of working alone each day in my studio, we were together. Upon Jake's request, I painted a killer whale in a green circle on the side of the bridge of his boat for protection when he hit the ocean—the fisherman's version of a St. Christopher medal. When the salmon ran, Jake went after them. He left on *The Gale* in tandem with his friend Bud on his boat Lady Luck for ten days.

Like a Portuguese fisherman's wife cruising the widow's walk, anticipating the return of her man, I sat on the dock at sunset and waited. I really missed him. Was I falling in love? When Jake landed, his boat laden with silver skinned slimy salmon, the scent of fish became the sweet smell of my lover's return.

He asked me to come on the next trip to Tomales Bay. No land law prevailed once we were twelve miles out. The idea of no restraints and the vista of the open sea made my life feel open to anything. The sea had textures and layers of color and motion you couldn't see from land. I used the railing as a ballet bar, finding new movements with the sway of the boat, my body overtaken by the wind and spray of salt water. The delicious flavor of freshly killed salmon cooked in the skillet on the boat's little burner stove released hundreds of taste buds I never knew I had. I learned to drive the boat because in the cabin I couldn't hear the sound of the hammer on the fish's head as it squirmed on the deck. I blocked out the brutality of it and just listened to the water and the radio.

I started smoking Camels unfiltered so I wouldn't smell Jake's cigarettes. I deluded myself into thinking I looked like a tough broad dragging on a fag who fit in with the fishing community instead of the delicate feminine young woman in flimsy sandals who didn't own a stitch of rugged clothing. After a couple of days, the diesel fumes began to get to me as did the need to paint. For months, we were together whenever he was on land and during my occasional trips to the sea.

∽

THINKING ABOUT THE SMELL OF SMOKE MAKES ME NAUSEOUS. I know I will never want to be near another cigarette, let alone light one. While two doctors near my bed talk about a sailing trip up to Block Island, I peer at them, squinting at the bright hospital lights. I can relax. They aren't approaching me.

∽

"I HAVE A GREAT SURPRISE," JAKE BEAMED. "I BOUGHT TWO Gloucester schooners converted to sardine packers in the 1930s. Bud and I are going to change them back to sailing fishing boats. They're 120 feet long, so there'll be plenty of room for you to paint in one of the holds. We can both do our thing. They are docked in Portland, Maine, and we're going up there to work on them."

"Whoa. First of all, why did you buy two?"

"One for me and one for Bud. He's been fishing commercially since he was a kid. He's second-generation and knows everything about fishing and sailing boats. He'll teach me how to work on them. Then think how cool it will be to sail around the world and have buddies on another boat."

"Sweetie, it's winter in Maine. You've never been to the East Coast. You have no idea how cold it is."

"It'll be great. You'll love everyone."

"Everyone?"

"Yeah. Bud is bringing that chick Shelley you introduced him to and Sunshine as crew. I asked my old friends Mike and Lois to be our crew. Of course, we'll bring Seth, my Lab, and your pooch, Sabaka. It'll be great. You and I can fly out. Mike and Lois will drive my Jeep."

"Huh? Who are these people?"

"Sunshine is an ex-Hell's Angel who has been crewing for Bud for years. You've seen him—long blond hair, blond beard, leather vest, lots of tattoos. He's a big softy but looks fierce. He'll keep us safe. I went to high school with Mike and Lois. They're good people. Mike can fix anything. Lois is his old lady. She's groovy."

"You planned everything and you expect me to follow you on this crazy adventure just like that?"

"Sorry, I thought you dug surprises. You're still coming, right?"

I saw the panic on his face as he laughed nervously, his hands in his pockets.

"How can I say no?" I was smitten with Jake and up for adventure as long as I could still paint.

He fiddled in his pocket and slowly pulled out a two-carat diamond ring. "Will you say yes to this too?"

Bombarded by surprises, I stared at the little rainbows on Jake's shirt reflected from the gem and at his face frozen in anticipation, the guy I didn't want to live without. The diamond triggered my early conditioning that life's main purpose was being a wife and mother, which I had thought I didn't want. Yet this particular whimsical man and going off to live with him on a big work-in-progress boat seemed too wonderful to pass up.

"Does that mean we have to get married?" I asked wanting to make sure it was adventure not indenture. At twenty-three, I was a feminist but shaved my legs.

"Not until you want to. I just want us to be together."

"Me too," I said to the man I would follow anywhere and with whom I might want to spend the rest of my life.

JIMMY AND JACQUES ENTER THE BURN UNIT WITH RED NOSES. MY brother touches my cheek with an icy finger, waking me up.

"You're so cold," I say.

"It's the March winds. No big deal. We just came by to say hi and drop off some chocolates. How are you? You look so young and peaceful. Oh yeah, the nurse gave us your mail."

He puts the get well cards on my table along with a postcard of Marcel Duchamp's painting of "The Bride." The inscription reads, "Mon Cherie Brahna, Life is full of surprises and there are good ones coming your way. Can't wait to see what you will be painting. A speedy recovery. Rose Selavy."

"Who do you think sent this?" I ask them. Jimmy and Jacques both shrug. I make a kissing motion with my lips. I'm not allowed mouth contact because of germs. It's lovely to see them, but my eyes close from wooziness. The chill on my cheek planted by the warmth of my brother takes my mind back to freezing Maine.

✍

EVERYTHING IN THE HARBOR OF PORTLAND WAS WHITE AND ICE, EXCEPT the water, spattered with countless chevrons of whitecaps. The docks resembled cross-country ski trails. The decks of the identical huge green-painted wooden ships were like ice skating rinks. The only vessels in the port each had an enclosed bridge with windows on three sides where the captain drove the boat with room enough to accommodate four seated passengers. It rose above the deck like a miniature penthouse with unobstructed views of sky and sea. This would be the crew's quarters. Several deep, dark fish holds looked like dungeons. Jake pointed to the largest one on his boat and said to me, "In a few months, this will be your studio."

"Looks a little dark, honey," I said, staring into the vague abyss. The rank smell of forty years of sardines drifted up my nose. "Let's close the hatch so no one falls in." I smiled.

The dusty Captain's quarters on each boat resembled those on *The Gale* except they were twice as large and had a potbelly stove for warmth and cooking.

The silver sky was huge and unobstructed by anything except twiggy branches of trees on the horizon's small islands. Through the ice floats, the slate gray water's depth appeared endless. The snow reflected an interior light, yet the bleakness and blasting cold winds made the deepest impact on us. Unlike Sausalito, we seven Californians were the waterfront scene.

Everyone looked at Jake in frozen amazement. "Are you kidding?" "You expect us to spend the winter here?" "When's the next plane back?" "Are you out of your mind?"

But his irrepressible enthusiasm convinced us all that we were living an adventure. Lobstermen pulled up to the boat several times a week selling their fresh catch for close to nothing. Bud and Jake spent endless days planning what they would do with the boats, but everything was frozen, and it was too cold to do any real work until the spring. Inside the cabin, it was cozy and warm. At night, my lover played the banjo, Mike the guitar, Lois the dulcimer. I read *War and Peace*, feeling calm and content with the gentle swaying of the boat, the music, foghorns outside. The town of Portland, the center of activity, was like a toy town from another century. The compact buildings looked like a vintage Christmas card. The streets bustled with people bundled in L.L. Bean clothes and boots running errands, working. Their red cheeks indicated the cold climate, yet they didn't hunch into themselves to keep warm as I did in defense of the sub-freezing temperature.

I rented a small studio in an artist building on the main street in Portland, walking distance to the dock, and spent days painting. I found some thin slabs of stone around the docks. I painted giant vertical cross sections of carrots, experimenting with the new materials and the convenient vegetable model. A couple of women, whose studio was down the hall, peeked in. "Wow, what a great feminist statement," one said. "Love that interior sexual image on the macho material surface." Although my artistic intent wasn't conscious, I welcomed the new friendship. No one else wanted anything to do with us because Patty Hearst had just joined the SLA in 1974, and the New Englanders mistrusted us Californians, thinking we had some remote connection. Living on their turf in anchored ships on the frozen water separated us from almost everyone.

At Christmas Jake brought a skinny pine tree into our cozy living space on the ship. Christmas was foreign to me. I had never had a tree. It was something Jewish families like ours didn't do. But what could be better than having one in Maine. Being part of the tradition in New England made me feel delightfully American. I made an aluminum foil Jewish Star to put on top to encompass my tradition of Chanukah.

"What do you do on Christmas?" I asked.

"You visit friends and wish good cheer," Jake replied. The water wasn't frozen over that day. Our little docked tribe that felt like family motored over to a nearby small island to visit a woman and her family who owned it. We drank eggnog and talked about boats and the weather. We gave her several cans of sardines. She gave us homemade preserves. I decided that I liked Christmas.

The rifle at dusk was the first thing I saw, but it didn't register at first. I had paintings on my mind as I approached Bud's boat at the dock.

"No trespassing," he said.

I froze. I couldn't tell if he was kidding. Even after spending months living in a floating commune together, I still couldn't figure Bud out. I had to cross his boat to get to ours, tied to the other side. Shelley stood next to him shivering in a flowered cotton long dress with a wool jacket over her, looking as if transplanted from a farm in a milder climate. Stepping close to me, she pointed a finger in my face and screamed, "Witch."

I had no idea where this came from. We were like sisters.

"Our territory. Keep moving. Get off our boat," Bud said, waving the rifle.

"Jake, Jake," I screamed.

My thick-soled snow boots helped me navigate the crunchy salted deck to the next boat. I felt Bud's rifle tip nudging my back and my heart about to jump out of my chest. Jake appeared in a second, grabbed me with one hand and the rifle with the other. I leaned into him. I saw he was trying to control himself, but his eyes were popping wildly with rage. I ran down below as he tilted his head in that direction. Crawling under the covers to stop shaking, I heard the voices above and Jake open the rifle, but no bullets fell out.

"Are you out of your fucking mind?" Jake said. "You scared the shit out of her. What's up with you, man, and with that chick of yours? I bought you a fucking boat. I thought we were bros. We had a plan. What's your problem?"

"We're done. Out of here. Tired of nothing to do. We're goin' home to California where I can fish. Just give me money to get us back and keep your damn boat. I don't want it."

"I had you all wrong. Start packing and get the hell out of here. Leave by tomorrow. I'll give you the bucks in a few."

Jake came down to the warm cabin and held me. "It's OK, babe, they're leaving. They turned into such freaks, and I think Shelley had a lot to do with it. She's probably jealous of you. She's such a lost chick. I hope we never see them again."

My shallow breath gained fullness. I felt protected and loved. Being able to think clearly I realized that Bud was the kind of guy who loved his independence. He was a hard-working fisherman who was always his own boss and wanted to go back to that. Jake's incredible generosity made us all dependent on him. Bud snapped.

"This is too heavy. Bud and Shelley are flipping out. Who's gonna be next? It's like falling into the depths of the hypothermic water that's surrounding us. Sweetie, can we get away from here for just a little while?" I said.

"You're right. I've had enough of these bad vibes, the cold, and feeling useless until the spring. Let's go to the Yucatan and hang out on some hammocks for a couple of weeks. Just you and me, baby. Lois, Mike, and Sunshine can hang out and watch the boats. They're cool here. By the time we return it should be warm enough to start working on them."

~

THE MORPHINE IS WEARING OFF AFTER MY LONG REVERIE. THE burning around my ankle where the doctor has stapled the skin graft feels like I am on fire again. I ring for the nurse who administers more sedation so I can live in the past.

~

WHEN WE RETURNED TO MAINE, JAKE CALLED IN ENGINEERS AND tradespeople who said that it would cost hundreds of thousands of dollars to convert the boats to functioning sailing fishing vessels. In their condition, they couldn't be moved further than Boothbay, Maine. The only thing to do was sell them and go back to California, leaving his losses behind.

Jake bought a couple of acres of land bordering on a state forest on the Willits Road near Ft. Bragg. It had two redwood Mongolian yurts connected by a stone path. We finally had a home together on firm ground. Each round structure had a diameter of 24 feet and rough-hewn redwood walls angled outward supporting a shingled roof with a large skylight in the center. From stone floor to skylight was eight feet. Small windows on the perimeter dotted the juncture of walls and ceiling less than six feet in height. Jake had to slouch until he got to the center, which made him feel like he was on the boat. One yurt was a bedroom, the other a living room and kitchen. Down a little path was a vegetable garden the previous owners installed, and along a path in the other direction was an outhouse. Jake had a light-filled rectangular studio built for me behind the bedroom yurt where I enjoyed the isolation of painting in nature. Yet it was a short ride to town to socialize with friends I had in the area from the time I lived in Mendocino a few years back.

My lover was gone for five days at a time and home for a few. The spirituality of the forest drew me in. The faces I noticed on the bark of the trees were my companions. I felt protected being surrounded by the strength and stability of the centuries of growth. Sitting on the ground carpeted with pine needles, the giant redwood I leaned against anchored me. I had recently learned I was pregnant. A new life grew inside my belly. I loved the feeling of being regenerative like nature. Yet I hadn't planned on having a baby at that point nor made plans for what would happen when it arrived. The newness of the situation made it an abstract event. There was no sense of time or the future, just the present. I figured we would work it out, somehow, without compromising our lifestyle. When the separation from Jake became unbearable, I went on the boat with him. He told me that after salmon season, he would be with me on land. I was joyous about the uninterrupted time we would have together. After a week in the yurts he said, "Tuna season starts next week. I'm going."

∽

I WAKE UP, LOOK AT MY BANDAGED BODY AND WONDER WHAT WILL happen now. My mother is keeping vigil by my bed. She is unconsciously scraping one manicured nail beneath another on her left hand – what she does while contemplating something. Seeing her in a familiar pose is comforting to me, and I drift off back to my conversation with Jake.

∽

"WE CAN'T MARRY IF YOU ARE ALWAYS AT SEA, AND I CERTAINLY can't be alone with a baby in the woods." The reality of our future pierced our little bubble. "That wasn't the plan," I screamed when he jumped off his boat on the dock after returning. He looked at my wet, swollen, red eyes and started crying too.

"I know, love. We wouldn't be happy together if you couldn't paint on land and I couldn't fish. And a kid?"

He sounded so rational I knew he had been thinking about us while on the water. At my request, he took me to the hospital in San Francisco for an abortion. Afterward we stayed in a fancy motel on Van Ness and ordered room service for two days. He held me in his arms like a delicate precious vase that he didn't want to drop or break. We clung onto each other and our love, while knowing the relationship would peel away, both relieved of not entering into a life neither of us was ready for.

Somewhere in my head while reliving the bittersweet ending of my time with Jake, I realized how lucky I was then. The relationship was perfect. When there was no way we could have moved it to the next level, which would have involved another human being, we parted without trauma, always loving what we had. He immersed himself in fishing and found a woman who had been a bear trapper. She also loved life as a commercial fisherwoman and later became his wife. I lived for my art.

∾

JUST AS I WAS FEELING SORRY FOR MYSELF, ANOTHER POSTCARD arrived—this time a Man Ray rayograph of two people kissing in profile. In the same flourishing script, it read, "Experiment, dear Brahna. Don't be afraid to go where no one else has gone. I can't wait to see what you come up with. Love, Man Ray." I knew that message referred to the new technique of photography he coined, but the kissing image made me sad. I couldn't imagine anyone wanting to kiss me. I couldn't imagine ever feeling not self-conscious enough to invite the opportunity. I drifted off to 1972 when I felt the opposite, the beams of attraction lighting my path.

Dozens of verdant shades filtered through the light on the Navarro River south of Mendocino. Nestled among giant ferns that looked like they had been there since the dinosaurs, under the tall redwoods, everyone hung out nude on the rocks and in the River enjoying the day. I didn't own a bathing suit then and doubted if anyone else did either. It was a scene reminiscent of centuries-old paintings of nymphs and beautiful young men like those of John William Waterhouse.

Another image enters my mind. In a purple leotard and long skirt after a dance class, feeling loose and energetic, I entered the Piewacket Cafe in Mendocino to grab something to eat. There he was, the bald, bushy browed, intense, dark-eyed legend visiting my town. I was flattered when Shel Silverstein nodded toward me, smiling slyly, and motioned to the chair next to him. Here was a famous older man who was determinately alternative, successful in writing songs, books, and articles for *Playboy*, and hung out with the sexiest women in America. I certainly didn't fit that stereotype, but the fact that he desired me made me feel like I was in that league and turned me on.

"You look like a local. Where's it happening tonight?" he said

"You're here," I answered, gesturing the room and encompassing our table in the wide sweep.

"I see. Just passing through to check out the scene and leavin' tomorrow. I have a groovy cabin on the cliff overlooking the ocean. The view is far out. Let me show you."

That was all it took. That's what fame did to me. I fantasized that maybe we could continue a friendship. Though a bit intimidated by his stature and satyr-like charm, I wanted to be memorable to him. In his little cabin with the background of the fierce Pacific waves pounding the rocks, I lay in his bed more attuned to his sexual pleasure than my own. I faked an orgasm during his, mimicking his howls simultaneously with him. Afterward he took out his guitar and played some of his songs for me. As if that wasn't enough, he said, "Hey, baby, I'm gonna change the lyrics of my song 'I Once Knew a Woman' so it's about you tonight." Then he sang, switching the eyes of the woman from brown to green like mine.

✧

I'M BROUGHT BACK TO THE PRESENT. I HEAR THE CURTAIN AROUND my bed rustle. Jimmy is approaching. Shaken out of my reverie, I show him the latest postcard of the kissing rayograph. "Who do you think is sending these? I'm dying to know. Is it Jorge? Ann? David? Who?"

"I'm not supposed to tell you because I thought you would have figured it out. It's Jacques. Don't tell him I told you. Make believe you guessed even though you didn't even include him in your list of possibilities. He just wanted to help you in some way, thought the postcards would boost your morale and encourage you to think about your art." I had never noticed Jacques's kindness underneath his fabulousness and now understood why Jimmy loved him deeply. I am grateful to have people who actively care and give me extra strength in my recovery.

3

DEPENDENT

"**M**AKE YOURSELF AT HOME," MY FATHER SAYS AS HE opens the door, using his body as a shield against brushing my tender skin against anything. After three months in the burn unit, I am moving into my parents' house in Brooklyn because I can't take care of myself—a dependent child again. I realize I have to start my life over, repeat becoming an adult, probably live differently. I have another chance at first experiences.

Yet there is too much clouding my optimism. It's 1983 and I haven't lived with them for eighteen years, more than half my life. After my brother and I left home, instead of downsizing, they moved to a larger, mid-century house in their neighborhood with pink tile bathrooms. It is totally unfamiliar to me. I never lived there. It's not like going home. It's like going backward, marking a new phase in my life.

It could be anyone's home but mine. True to my mother's nature, everything has a designated place. There isn't a stray piece of paper in sight. My childhood houses were fanatically organized, but this house brings that organization to its zenith aided by built-in mahogany cabinets and fitted closets in every room. The architect, also a yachtsman, modeled the house's efficiency of space on that of a ship, complete with an anchor on the front lawn.

My parents' house is the antithesis of my loft, which is all open space with the exception of my small bedroom. The largest storage area I have is a niche built into the wall for my paintings.

❧

JUST TWO AND A HALF YEARS BEFORE, I HAD ARRIVED IN TRIBECA and stayed with Jimmy and Jacques before I found my own loft in one of the many warehouses where artists lived and worked. Before I began my search, my mother called, her voice squealing with excitement because I had returned from over a decade in California. Her theory of family was keeping her children on a rubber band that would snap back to her when it reached its limit. I had boomeranged home after twelve years.

"Sweetheart," she said almost breathlessly, "wouldn't you rather live in one of those gorgeous brownstones in the Village? If I moved back to the city that's where I would want to live. We could buy one for a steal in this market." New York City real estate was at an historic low. The city was financially a mess and generally not safe.

Cringing on my side of the phone, I said, "Ma, I'm not you. I want to get a loft and one I can afford to rent on my own, OK?"

"Are you sure you wouldn't rather be in the Village? There aren't any stores to shop for food or clothes or anything down there. What about a dry cleaner? It's so deserted."

"Ma-a-a... Anyway, Jimmy lives here so don't worry." How could I explain to her that Tribeca's grime was glamorous? Just being down there I felt on the fringe of society yet on the edge of something about to happen. There wasn't any crime in Tribeca because it was still a working warehouse district, and burglars and muggers didn't know anyone lived there. Most taxi drivers didn't know where it was. The only residents were artists and creatives. It was exactly where I wanted to be, and rents were dirt cheap.

Having given it her best shot, she immediately went into high gear organizing my loft search. An expert list maker, she combed the *Village Voice* compiling daily itineraries. Her efficiency reminded me of how I hated to make lists and how as a child I tried to fulfill the unwritten list of what my parents and grandparents expected of their nice Jewish girl. A constant accessory to the kitchens of my youth was a white plastic wall dispenser spewing a narrow roll of paper, a pen dangling on a chain beside it. There my mother inscribed in her perfect penmanship a running list that extended from the dispenser like slightly unraveled toilet paper. Something always needed to be done or bought. I suppose by itemizing her tasks, it made the overwhelming responsibilities of being a young mother and wife manageable for her. It was all those enumerated things to do and the years dedicated to fulfilling them that made me want more than a life of taking care of my family's minutia, as my mother so lovingly did.

Returning years later to Manhattan, I was impressed and grateful for my mother's help and efficient commandeering of my search for a home. She had circled everything in my price range in Tribeca and Soho and made appointments for us.

We approached a small corner building with "coffee" painted high on the brick facade near the roof, indicating its recent use as a warehouse for the beans. It was the real deal. When I saw the open loft with walls of windows, I inhaled the eleven hundred square feet with a deep breath.

"Perfection! Look at this light," I said to the real estate broker and grinned giddily at my mother standing by my side. The six windows facing north provided steady light all day and looked out at the loading docks of the Summit Import Company warehouse. The truck wheels bouncing on the cobblestone street provided a rumbling white noise. I looked forward to hearing that sound as the undertone to my cassettes of Lou Reed and the Velvet Underground, Tom Waits, and Miles Davis.

The four western windows faced the Hudson River. Noting the wind and sun patterns streaming across the water from the unhampered view, I said, "I'll take it." I had enough money saved from my jobs and selling all my possessions—including my car— to pay the one-time $6,000 fixture fee, a standard component in renting a loft. This space had been a clothes designer's studio. It had a very basic Pullman kitchen with a small refrigerator under the counter and a bare bathroom with toilet, sink, and shower. Most of it was open space, so I could think and paint. There was a huge closet where she had stored her clothes. It was big enough for my bed and a dresser.

"If this makes you happy, fine by me. It's a nice place to paint, but where will you sleep and eat?" my mother asked in her Lord & Taylor slacks and blazer.

"Don't mind me," she added, addressing the broker. "I'm just here to keep my daughter company. The decision is all hers."

I uttered a silent "yes!" beneath my breath. Relieved to hear her small declaration, it confirmed to me that I had returned to New York City as an adult free to make my own choices. The Brooklyn Bridge separated me from the censorships and restrictions acquired growing up in Manhattan Beach.

❧

BUT THREE AND A HALF YEARS AFTER THAT THRILLING DAY OF GETTING MY loft, that's exactly where I ended up. My parents' master suite was on the first floor. They designated the upstairs guest bedroom for me.

"Hey, baby, it's so good to have you here," my father said as he

brought my things up to the second floor. "You're my F. L., you know."
F. L. was our code for first love, meaning first born. He called me that
when he wanted me to know how special I was to him. My mother
trailed us as I followed him up the stairs. The first stairs I navigated
in three months, I moved slowly and watched my balance.

My father dumped my bags willy nilly around the room. Light
gray painted bamboo textured wallpaper covered the walls. A
built-in wood unit of black shelves and desk occupied a corner
where Jimmy had studied for his bar exam. A door opened onto a
wraparound terrace. I followed my mother's stare at the disarray on
the floor and realized my bags were the only things not contained in
an organized compartment. I was afraid of creating disorder in my
parents' house and didn't know how I could prevent it since I was
the embodiment of physical transition.

As my mother arranged my clothes, bandages, and ointments
on shelves, I laid down on the narrow single bed on top of a quilted
coverlet of gray, black, and white circles and tried to ignore my
itchy skin. I felt like I had jet lag—exhausted from the drive and
light headed by the early summer fresh air after confinement in the
hospital since early March. I watched the shadows on the rug cast by
the afternoon light through the mosque-like decorative iron window
grates. The slanting lines and overlapping circles mesmerized me.
Then with an unnoticeable shift of the sun, they suddenly vanished,
returning the rug to its uniform gray tweed. I twitched as if I had
just had an electric shock at the unanticipated change in the room
and feared not knowing what would happen next in the moment or
in the future. I named my chamber the gray room.

After I finally fell asleep, I woke myself with a scream, my skin
burning with pain. My stomach turned, doomed, knowing my
life would never be the same. My father ran upstairs and held me
gingerly. His shoulders hunched over his six-foot frame. His eyes
were wide and an unfamiliar crease appeared between his eyebrows.
He had always been the one who did something to fix a situation.
But he couldn't fix this. "Hi, gorgeous," he said. Did you hear the
one about the Rabbi, Priest, and Minister who walked into a bar?"
and proceeded with the joke. This was his way of coping.

The house, a half block from the ocean, became a harbor of
safety where my well-being was constantly attended to. Little did I
know that what I thought was a temporary retreat would serve as an
aquatic haven in future decades. After my mother and father died, I—
the lone survivor—spent the entire summer of 2016 in Manhattan

Beach, emptying their house of the artifacts and furnishings of four generations of family.

Crossing the sand, the sea air cleansed my lungs. The scene at the beach had changed since my youth. Standing in the slick wet sand, a Muslim woman shrouded from head to ankles waded in the water up to her knees. Orthodox Jewish boys with paes flying ran past with wet mud in their pails to build sand castles. Bare-breasted women covered in tattoos lounged on blankets. I entered the ocean past a couple embracing, only their faces above water, their mouths glued together; past muscular boys tossing a ball; teenagers with shower caps standing in waist high water; children splashing each other; a woman swimming by in a rhinestone baseball cap and sunglasses asking me in a Russian accent if I knew the time. I swam past these distractions, past the discarded plastic bags and cups and other detritus out to where it was empty and clean. I stretched my aching body. Halfway to the next jetty my mind cleared and I floated.

When I walked back to the house to shower and lock up, I pictured my father in his old age sitting in the den waiting for me to take him out to dinner and asking me, "How was the water?" And I would describe the waves, the level of cleanliness and particular beach crowd of the day. No matter what my answer, he'd say, "I'm glad you had a good swim." The past comfort of their house as an adult starting from my recovery never left me.

Swimming at Manhattan Beach helped me cope with tragedies that happened in the world outside myself. On 9/11, although lucky to be unharmed, we had to escape Tribeca and could not return to our loft for a couple of weeks. We sought refuge with my parents out of the city in Manhattan Beach. During those hot weeks in September when the world had changed, each day filled with uncertainty, our country and us, its citizens, experienced an unprecedented vulnerability. I found some peace walking over to the deserted beach. I would never have imagined that my way of dealing with a personal disaster would be palliative for the magnitude of this public one nineteen years later. I swam the length of the beach from rock jetty to rock jetty, submerged in the ocean, and while counting my strokes, found comfort in the water, removed from disaster and a world where I had no control.

∽

BACK IN 1982, PROTECTED IN MY PARENTS' HOME, I DIDN'T HAVE to deal with the everyday chores of paying bills, sorting out health insurance, or buying and preparing food. I didn't have to explain my changed appearance to friends and acquaintances.

Yet I cringed from embarrassment when my mother carefully sponged my raw back in the shower before asking her to leave the bathroom so I could continue washing the rest of my body. The water on my red skin stung as the scabs peeled off and vanished down the drain. I didn't wear my contact lenses in the shower. Any more clarity on my blurry image would have been intolerable. I wrapped myself in a soft towel. Mom waited in the gray room.

I took a deep breath before exposing myself again when she applied the ointments and gauze to the parts of my body I couldn't reach due to the lack of mobility of my right arm. I was grateful for her tender competence but hated feeling helpless once more when I had to shout down the stairs, "Ma, can you come up and help me with this button," frustrated at not being able to dress myself when I thought I had selected something so easy to put on.

❧

I HAD FLASHBACKS TO 22 GIRARD STREET, WHERE WE LIVED UNTIL I was twelve, just down the block from my parents' current house. It was that memory of home that appeared in my dreams and thoughts. As a child, while my father and grandfather spent long days at work, my mother and grandmother reigned in the two-family house we shared.

Grandma Celia was the driving force of the matriarchy. She was my life raft. When I was two, my grandma took me to Brighton Beach, a respite from our hot Manhattan Hell's Kitchen apartments. As we trudged to the water, dodging people's towels, screaming beach-goers and blaring AM radio stations, she put me on her back to avoid the hot sand burning my feet. She plowed into the crowded ocean. "Now ve svim," she said in her Russian accent. "Don't let go of my neck." Riding on her back, I bobbed in the water, the cool waves splashing over me, the security of her body beneath me as she did the breast stroke. I pressed my body to her back like a permanent hump, squealing at the excitement of buoyancy. I never wanted to leave the water or her. A year later my grandparents bought the two-family house in more upscale, secluded Manhattan Beach.

Around that early age, Grandma Celia started her mantra. "Find a boy who wants to be a doctor. We'll pay for medical school. Find a boy who wants to be a doctor. We'll pay for medical school." It sounded like a lullaby. She chanted this as I snuggled into her

48

fleshy smooth olive-skinned arms while sunning on her porch. In her kitchen on the top floor of our house, she spread wax paper over the table and took out flour, a mixing bowl, eggs, jam, and a rolling pin. "I'm going to teach you to make rugelach," she said. "I know you are a smart girl, but you shouldn't worry about going out and making a living. We want you to have a good life and not struggle like we did. Marry a professional—a doctor. I'll teach you to be a balabooster. Have some children, live in a nice big house, and you'll be happy." That's when the meaning of the mantra hit. She assumed I would find fulfillment by serving and helping a man achieve his glory and dreams as she did with my grandfather.

I preferred to hang out in my bedroom, walls covered by pink wallpaper with interlocking patterns of birds and leafy branches. I liked to stare at the patterns and make sketches of different parts of them. If I stared long enough, I would see colored dots and paramecium shapes overlaying everything and draw them.

I secreted a blue-covered book of Picasso's life with reproductions of his art under my bed. I took it out and hid it under my skirt. I ran to the bathroom where I could lock the door and no one would disturb me settling in to look at the pictures as if they were pornography. I didn't tell how much I wanted the artist's life, where society didn't dictate how I should live. At twelve, I thought I would seek out a great artist, like Picasso, and be his mistress. What could be more exciting? After reading about the tragic lives of Picasso's women, I realized I wanted to be the great artist. But was that possible? I had never heard of any famous women artists except Mary Cassatt. My mother had a book of her paintings in the kitchen. When I flipped through the pages, all I saw were paintings of mothers and children. The subject matter reflected my mother's life, not one I was interested in living or painting. I wanted to create things that no one had seen before, get my hands dirty, and live among free spirits in a place foreign to me.

At dinner I held up the book to my mother and said, "I see you like Mary Cassatt's paintings. I think . . . "

"Put that book down or you'll end up like my friend Bernie," my father interrupted.

"What's wrong with Bernie?" I asked

"He's hardly got any patients is what's wrong with him," he said. "Up all night, always with the art hobby. He's too tired in the morning to be a podiatrist."

Since my mother didn't comment over dinner, the next day I proudly showed her my sketches. "Beautiful," she said. "You are good at so many things, but don't you think you should go outside and get some fresh air?"

I rode my bike across the street from our house along the bay on the peaceful peninsula where nothing exciting ever happened or changed.

Walking on Shore Boulevard one day with my friend Arlene I felt especially bored. We passed the red firebox that sat on a short pole on the corner. "What do you think would happen if I pulled down the red lever?" I asked her. "I don't know, but you're not supposed to, unless there's a fire," she said. I never did anything I wasn't supposed to do and I just wanted to see what it would be like. I pulled the lever. I felt the thrill of the forbidden for about five seconds. When we heard the fire engines, Arlene ran home, and I ran into our house and hid in my room, shaking with fear that the doorbell would ring and I'd be taken to jail for distracting the firemen from a real emergency.

The next Sunday at Arlene's house, her mother invited me to stay for a dairy dinner—bagels, lox, sturgeon, and sable. I loved that Jewish soul food. I called my mother, whose predicted answer was, "Are you sure it's OK?" "They invited me, Mom," I whispered into the phone. "OK, then. Be good and don't stay too long." Sitting around the circular table in the breakfast room, I couldn't take my eyes off Arlene's dad. I wasn't used to being around friends' fathers. They were never home, always at work doing important things, and this one was a judge! I was intimidated. Staring and imagining him sitting on a high bench looking down on people who stood below and deciding their fate, even sending them to be fried in the electric chair like the Rosenbergs, was the scariest thing I could think of. What if he knew about the false alarm? What would my punishment be? The fear of disaster roiled in my stomach when I looked across the table at the short balding middle-aged man hunched over his plate, engrossed in the smoked fish. I don't think he even noticed I was there because I didn't utter a peep, so in awe of his power I could hardly swallow. When I left, Arlene's mom asked if I had enough to eat and said I was a sweet girl. I was known for being a sweet girl.

Aware of the blanket of expectations that covered the thirty blocks of our bay to ocean community, McCarthyism, the Cold War, the Beats, and Abstract Expressionism were only words and images to me from *Life Magazine*. None of this entered our world only a half hour out of Manhattan. It was a world where at the beginning of every season, my mother came home from her excursion to Bonwit Teller, in the City, and covered my bed with blouses, skirts and dresses. I happily picked the matching outfits that I liked the most, making sure I never had to wear the same thing twice in a week

✍

AT MY PARENTS' HOUSE, RECOVERING FROM THE FIRE, I REALIZED that my body didn't remember the recent severe pain. I could use words to describe it, but as a tool of preservation my body itself blocked out the sensation. It had been the only reality that captured my attention for months, and it took over every nerve and fiber of my being, obliterating all thoughts because of its intensity. I was relieved to understand the nature of extreme pain. I couldn't function in the present if I relived it. My brain now had a vast space to experience thoughts, observations, problem solving, other sensations. My memories of childhood became more selective and sweeter. Just as in the past, the summer air was thick with a salty breeze stirring the humidity, mixed with the rich musty green scent of the leafy mature trees that marked the neighborhood. That clear, pure smell expanded my lungs, filled my deep breath.

✍

WHEN I WAS LITTLE, WE SPENT HOURS DURING THE SUMMER ON the back porch off my bedroom at 22 Girard Street. I sat on my father's lap in my one-piece pale pink bathing suit covered with lines of gingerbread men holding hands topped by a little pink ruffle below the shoulder straps. My father counted the beauty marks on my arm and back. "One," he whispered with a little poke. "Two," he said a little louder with a tiny pinch. "Three," he said even louder, tickling me. When he reached seven, his voice was triumphant, his fingers moving as fast as a piano virtuoso, tickling me full speed under my arms, my back and tummy. I laughed so hard he had to hold tight or I would have fallen on the cement porch floor. My mother, in halter-top and shorts sang "Summertime." As a teenager, she had been a singer on the radio, but at seventeen chose my father's marriage proposal over that of being in the spotlight of a big band. Her beautiful, slow, deep voice was the sound of her love. The still air smelled of honeysuckle, and cool drops of water sprayed from the lawn sprinkler as she crooned.

✍

IN THEIR CURRENT HOUSE WE HAD DINNER ON THE SHADED PATIO off the formal dining room. Sitting at the old wrought iron table with the glass top from our collective past, I needed to have pillows to cushion the delicate burned skin on my back against the hard wrought iron chairs.

"Please sing 'Summertime,' Mom," I asked in the warm evening, no longer scented by honeysuckle. "Summertime and the livin' is easy . . . With mommy and daddy standing by."

I didn't look at my body in a full-length mirror for months, not wanting to see who replaced the me I had known. After applying moisturizer on my face, I clumsily lifted my right arm to insert my contact lenses, my mangled limb of multiple textures resembling a manhole cover didn't appear human to me. My fingers and hands were prematurely crinkled and discolored with patches of red and white. Even my finger prints were gone, and I couldn't avoid catching the reflection in the small medicine cabinet mirror of the scar on my neck, a red taut rope, making it an effort to turn my head away.

In my parents' house, I had access to too many mirrors and assessed the superficial collateral damage besides the burns. My face and body were puffy from three months of lying in a hospital bed. The fire had singed my long hair, the damaged clumps chopped off in the burn unit. In the protective custody of my parents, my weird hair was one more thing that freaked me out about my appearance.

"This we can fix," my mother said with a smile. That simple phrase had a familiar ring. Growing up I knew I could count on her to make things right if I couldn't do it myself. She called a local beautician to the house to even out my straggly locks. The result was a shorter, feathered cut with a potential for puffiness ready to be styled into Brooklyn big hair, one small step toward general normalcy and one step away from my image of myself as a downtown artist.

My mother's efforts to make me feel more comfortable were undeniable. When given the chance, she was the ultimate nurturer. Living in her home, we fell into our primal pattern. I took it for granted that she was there to help me get through this phase of my recovery. She gave herself unconditionally to me—the same little girl who started wearing glasses at four, my mother had understood my embarrassment when called four eyes because she had suffered the same fate. She made sure I had cool plaid or checked frames so the glasses became a fashion accessory. At thirteen she took me to her optometrist to be fitted for contact lenses. Together, we now faced the biggest challenge yet.

4

OUTPATIENT

EACH MORNING MY MOTHER TOASTED A BAGEL FOR ME and set out a platter of freshly sliced nova lox and Philadelphia cream cheese before Sol from car service drove me into the city for my daily six hours of physical and occupational therapy at St. Vincent's Hospital. Her nourishing ritual fortified me to face the day. Under any other circumstances, a driver would have been an unthinkable luxury, but it was my parents' solution for necessary transport; my father worked in New Jersey, my mother didn't drive in the city. Sitting in the back of Sol's Lincoln, each pothole was another assault on my traumatized body slamming against the seat. I did not feel privileged.

∽

I HAD TO LEARN TO REBUILD MY MUSCLES TO REGAIN USE OF MY painting arm. The therapists chatted among themselves as I exercised on machines that reminded me of the ones I painted in my *Man/Machine* series before the accident. I thought about my opening of that art exhibit while going through my exercises in occupational therapy.

∽

SIX-FOOT BY SIX-FOOT PAINTINGS LINED THE GALLERY'S WALLS. I arrived early and had to lean against the door frame for a moment until my dizziness passed. I tried taking deep breaths, but the air wouldn't budge below my throat. What if people didn't like the work? What if no one showed up? One canvas depicted massive thighs and a segment of the machine between them. Another was a giant bicep with its elbow resting on the pad of the machine. Although my technique was hyper-realistic, by omitting the face and a good portion of the rest of the body, the paintings had an abstract quality and composition. "What is the meaning of these paintings?" asked the first visitors to the show. My answer, which I had already given in a press release, was, "I want to juxtapose human strength against a mechanized impersonal society." At that point, I was too excited and nervous to engage in a lengthy discussion.

A real body builder in a Speedo stood on a platform in the middle of the room. Initially, I thought it was a cheap publicity stunt by the gallery owners, giving the exhibit a side show quality. Then I realized that he didn't take anything away from the work and his presence contributed to the energy of the room. In contrast to him and my paintings, I looked like a fragile bird. My cropped dark hair was spiked. I had methodically checked out every Soho shop that I loved until I found a hand-painted white wool short dress with splashes of reds, purples, and blues. It clung to my body without being tight and made me feel sophisticated, sexy, and arty. I splurged on a pair of purple Bennis Edward high-heeled ankle boots.

The gallery filled quickly, leaving people to linger outside creating a buzz. As I squeezed through the crowd, I heard snippets of conversation in the packed room. "Man becomes more like the machine he wrestles with" "The impressionist palette is wonderfully ironic." They're actually getting it, I thought. The paintings are touching them. This was my moment.

Jimmy, Jacques, and their friends descended on me, with bundles of flowers.

"Fabulous work, darling." "Stunning." "You look gorgeous."

I felt gorgeous, fabulous, and stunning and the most confident I had ever been in my life. My dealers took my elbow, introducing me to clusters of people. Dazzled by being the center of attention, I assumed the gallery owners found it necessary to exhibit the artist as well as the art. I smiled. The best part was that by making the surfaces look very real, I created a world I could control.

My mother beamed. My father looked dapper in his turtle neck and tweed sports jacket and nodded his head in approval as he lifted his plastic cup filled with champagne to toast me across the room. I noticed a perplexed wrinkle on his brow when he scrutinized the paintings.

Just one painting sold because it seemed that when it came down to actually living with large paintings of male body parts, people had a hard time committing. Bloomingdale's rented the paintings for their windows as a background for bathing suit-clad mannequins. A posh Upper East Side gym rented them for their offices and public areas. This was far from my ideal audience and did not fulfill my highest hopes for the show. However, I gained a few good reviews and a following of people who understood the work but whose apartments and finances were too small for it. The revenue from the show and what I had left from the sales of the parachute works bought me almost another year of painting time. Eating mainly brown rice and occasionally painting theater sets, I was surviving as an artist in New York City—in my mind, a great beginning.

~

AS AN OUTPATIENT I FELT LIKE ANOTHER SPECIES COMPARED TO the therapists. Yet they didn't treat me as an alien. "You're looking good today." "Let's increase the weight." "One more rep. You're getting stronger."

I would have been happy to trade places with any of these women who were around my age. Each had the armor of a diamond on her left fourth finger, which came with a man to buffer her against the world. As I went through my paces, I wondered if I would ever have a husband to run interference for me. Not that I thought I wanted one or needed one before the accident. Would I ever want anyone to see my body? Would I ever have a man who found me attractive and wanted to share a life? Would I have the physical and emotional strength to do meaningful work that made me happy as the work these therapists had? I was a voyeur to people who enjoyed their lives—lives I never would have previously wanted. I had the cool life—painting all day and hanging out at the Odeon or downtown clubs at night. I surprised myself at my mundane desires compared to my past aspirations of making it in the art world. Yet I also realized that it was ridiculous to label a life mundane if it was fulfilling. What I really wanted was unlimited options.

My exhaustion made me feel like silly putty inside, though I moved like a wind-up doll running out of batteries. I used to move like a dancer. Now the stiffness of my own shadow shocked me. After occupational therapy, I entered a small, too brightly fluorescent-lit room. Merry, my jovial physical therapist in a white doctor's coat that was too small for her, stretched me while I laid on a sheet-covered mat on the floor. She used all her weight exerting extra pressure on my right side. Merry pulled my legs to the right and instructed me to move my torso and head to the left, an unfathomable goal due to the scar that descended down my neck to my right shoulder. Then she moved me in the opposite direction, wringing me out like a rag. I thought how easily I did this yoga stretch before the fire, how good it felt then, how hard it was now.

"Hold onto my arms," she said as she leaned over and dragged me along the mat. Her heft supported me. I fixated on the skin of her flawless, smooth, soft forearms, something I would never have, making them even more beautiful to me. She never stopped smiling or wavering from her focus. Wearing two hospital gowns, one tied in the back and another one over it tying in the front, I laid on my back across a big green rubber ball. With my blue spongy hospital-slipper feet trying to anchor the ground, Merry pulled my arms over my head aiming for the floor behind me. I brought my camera to therapy after a few months. I wanted my therapist to take pictures of me over the ball and laying on the mat, visualizing a series of self-portraits I would paint in the future when I could use my arm again.

Reaching up to grab the chinning bar was as difficult as touching the ceiling. Once I had my fingers wrapped around the bar, I hung for a few torturous minutes. Merry was there to catch me if I fell. "No pain, no gain," she said in a sing-song voice. "My husband is making pasta tonight with his killer clam sauce with fresh clams, garlic, oregano, Parmesan cheese." I salivated holding onto that bar just imagining the taste. "If we have any leftovers I'll bring some in for you." I knew she wouldn't. It was her technique to distract me and keep me from letting go.

❧

WHEN MOST OF THE SCABS HAD FALLEN OFF FROM THE SKIN GRAFTS, six months after the fire, my mother and I visited Dr. Haher in her office a block from the Metropolitan Museum. Soft-colored landscapes in ornate frames hung on the light pink walls. "Look, you can put on the hospital gown yourself! I see you've been working hard at physical therapy. Keep it up. You'll be painting soon." she said. Buoyed by this thought I noticed a painting on her wall of a woman walking down a road with the signature "Haher."

"Is that recent?" I asked, lifting my right arm as much as possible in its direction.

"Yes, but it took forever because I don't get to paint very often. Not like you who will be doing it full time again. I envy you that."

She surveyed my body. I would feel like a piece of meat under anyone else's scrutiny but hers. As she ran her fingers over my arms and inspected my back she said, "You are improving nicely, now we need to smooth out the scar tissue. You'll have to wear scar compression garments for at least a year. I know it's tedious, but eventually, you'll be able to wear three quarter sleeves and no one will notice." Her certainty about my future made me optimistic about the next step. Not seeing myself as a burn victim consumed me.

My mother accompanied me to the dreary offices of a surgical supply company where they would fit me with scar compression garments called Jobst. Her furrowed forehead and widening eyes behind her glasses reflected her dread of yet another ordeal in my healing process-the same pained look on her face I had seen in the hospital.

I knew her suffering because I was suffering.

Yet every bit of my energy focused on holding myself together and going through the pain and drudgery of rehabilitation to resemble a woman I would be able to accept. Reading my mind, she whispered to me as we were escorted down the gray hall, "This too shall pass."

In the dressing room, I removed my clothes to be instructed how to put on the four part, tighter than skin ensemble. The top piece, a long-sleeved "jacket" covering my torso, from my hips to under my chin, had round circular cups demarcated with zigzag stitching for my breasts. It zipped up the front. If only it were leather it would have an S & M coolness, but I was the opposite of a dominatrix— my scarred skin looked as if it has been flayed by a brutal whipping.

"Let me help you," my mother said as I struggled to step into the bottom half, a combination legging and girdle. I shook my head no. It took an arduous half hour as I inched it up to my waist, wrinkle by wrinkle. The gloves, two sizes smaller than my usual size 7, were essential in flattening the ridges on my fingers and back of hand. The fourth piece was a little cap with a strap on each side that attached together with Velcro under my chin. The tighter the pressure, the flatter the scars along my jawline leading to my neck would become. I pulled the Velcro so hard I had trouble swallowing. I put my clothes on over my new under garments.

"Do you want to have lunch before we go home?" my mother asked. The only thing I could imagine making its way down my compressed throat was ice cream, and I didn't want to be in a restaurant sporting my new gear that I had to wear all the time except for showering. We returned to Brooklyn.

THE DOORBELL RANG. AUNT SYLVIA BUSTLED IN DECKED OUT IN her jewels and high heels toting a Bloomingdale's shopping bag.

"Darling, you must have had quite a day," she said as she grabbed my hand. "I see you're wearing the whatcha-ma-call-it."

"Jobst," I said, sitting stiffly in the den.

"You've got to try on these things. It'll perk you right up." She pulled one silk garment out of her bag after another, like a magician with scarves in a hat. Her legendary closets were full of clothes she had never worn; many still had sales tags, so it was not quite clear if these were all recent purchases. Sylvia, whose favorite color was blue, especially turquoise, was a couple of sizes larger than I was, so I found myself swimming in a turquoise sea of Yves St. Laurent, Pierre Cardin, Diane B silk, cotton, and linen blouses, skirts, and scarves. I didn't recognize myself in the mirror wearing my new wardrobe. Without Aunt Sylvia's enthusiasm, I would have felt like a clown instead of the camouflage queen she was helping me to become, hiding everything except my face.

"Brahna" she cooed, "that color is fabulous on you. It makes you come alive. Aren't I right? The polka-dotted scarf can be your trademark." Her black eyeliner crinkled in a familiar smile and made me think that maybe I looked OK. I trusted her. My favorite aunt had taken me to see "Golden Boy," my first Broadway show, at seven. Theater and lunch at Sardi's became an ongoing tradition.

"I went out with Harry last night; thank you for asking," she said. "Who's Harry?"

"We met at the spa in Miami Beach. I told you in the hospital."

"Sorry, I was in a morphine delirium."

"Well, anyway, look at these gorgeous earrings he bought for me. You like?"

"What a cool way of using opals," I said, noting the mosaic of iridescent opal chips that formed silver dollar-sized discs covering her ear lobes. They matched her opal pendant and ring.

My skin itched beneath the Jobst, and I knew I shouldn't rub my back against the couch because it would result in permanent puckering of my skin. I longed for the distraction of her story.

"I prefer the company of dignified older men. Not the young gigolos that gave massages at the spa. Some of those women went in for that. Can you imagine paying! Not me."

"How old is Harry?"

"Eighty and smart as a whip. A retired attorney. He keeps his mind sharp by playing bridge."

"So where did you go?"

"He picked me up in his white Caddy, and we went local to Lundy's in Sheepshead Bay. You know how much I love lobster," she said, licking the corner of her mouth unconsciously, and smiled with contentment.

"Are the waiters still black men with white gloves?" I asked, remembering the restaurant of my youth. I remembered the weird colonial atmosphere but could taste their delicious signature soft biscuits and lobster.

"No, it hasn't been like that for ages. Anyway, then we came back to my house and played gin rummy because I don't know how to play bridge. He's very attentive and such a gentleman."

She winked and gave me an air kiss so she wouldn't smudge her lipstick. She tottered out the door and down the block to her house, leaving the den with the scent of her tea rose perfume. I loved that smell. It made me think of silk scarves and ladies with big hats meandering through opulent gardens.

I heard sneezing. "Has Sylvia left?' my mother said, approaching the den. "I love my sister dearly, but she knows I'm allergic to that perfume, and she insists on wearing it when she comes over." I found comfort and humor in the little quibbling between them, basking in the security of family and their attention in this separate world where nothing was demanded of me, except to recover.

〰

WHEN MY FATHER CAME HOME FROM WORK HE PLAYED HARRY Belafonte and joined in singing "Day-o, day-o" off key to create a fun atmosphere and remind me of when I was a kid in simpler times. I grew up with Broadway musicals. My father, a sales manager for a firm that manufactured TV antennas, had an expense account for out-of-town customers. Whenever Mr. and Mrs. Smith had to cancel, my parents took Jimmy and me to see "The Music Man," "Oklahoma," "Can Can," "The Sound of Music."

I thought back to when I first settled in Tribeca. One of my jobs was painting scenery in theaters off Broadway. In my green industrial painters' jumpsuit, I loved creating large-scale illusions like wood-paneled walls and sky outside of windows in make-believe rooms. Working with a scenic designer and backstage crew balanced working alone in my studio. What could be more New York than working in the theater! I planned to take the scenic painting union exam down the line as an insurance policy for a living wage—my back-up in case my own art didn't always support me. Now, my damaged arm erased that option.

↶

THAT NIGHT I WOKE UP SCREAMING AGAIN, FEELING THE PRESSURE, constriction and unfamiliarity in the encasement of the Jobst. My mother rushed upstairs.

"I had a dream about you, darling," she said. "We were at your wedding. You were marrying a very handsome man. His name was Stuart."

"What kind of dream is that, Ma? You think I'll marry someone named Stuart?"

"It could happen," she answered as I hoisted myself up wrapping my arms around her and kissing her soft cheek.

If dreams were premonitions, I wanted to believe in hers.

5

CAMOUFLAGE

VENTUALLY, THE DAILY ROUTINE AND THE ISOLATION from anyone who didn't have something to do with the repair of my body began to depress me. I wanted to participate more in the world, besides going to the hospital daily and being a work in progress. I applied to an art therapy program at the New School across the street from St. Vincent's Hospital while still living at my parents' home. The admissions requirements were to show the instructor, an impressive, tall, blond woman with a big brain and low cut blouse, slides of my work. I showed her the *Man/Machine* series. "How interesting that before the accident you painted fragments of bodies," she said in a German accent, pointing to the painting of a chest and arms pulling the bicep machine. "I especially think this one is a remarkable premonition of what was to come because the colors and surface of the skin are so unnatural." I wondered how she knew about my skin's surface and colors. After all, I was wearing my signature scarf and camouflage clothes.

After hours of my own therapy stretching and contorting my body, I attended class, scarf dramatically wrapped around my neck, grateful the other students were strangers. Humbled by the fire and inspired by the physical therapists dedicated to my recovery, I wanted to heal other people as well as myself.

At night in my bedroom in my parents' house, I read Jung, Freud, and Edith Kramer for the class. I gravitated to Jung's theory of the collective unconscious of pre-existing images. We inherit these different archetypes as part of our humanity. This gave a psychological name to images I had seen repeated in different ways by many artists and to the power that drew me to choose the ones I used myself. In the next few months, few years, and into the present, Jung's idea that the cause of behavior was past experiences in addition to future aspirations became part of the lexicon of my being. Edith Kramer, the founder of art therapy, combined art-making with Freud's concept of sublimation: the process in which urges arising from the id transform into socially productive and acceptable outcomes that gratify the original urge. I remembered all my nights of putting my sexual feelings into my parachute paintings and now could see them in the context of having practiced art therapy on myself. I saw it everywhere in the art world. I would eventually witness Kramer's theories blatantly displayed when I would work with children and adults who had problems controlling basic urges and I helped them harness them into art.

We were required to make drawings or watercolors. I couldn't control a brush, water, and paint yet. I gingerly picked up a colored pencil. My hand was not very flexible in holding something so narrow. The lines I made were tentative and tended to waver. After many attempts, my fingers were finally strong enough to create perceptible images. Although the drawings were somewhat child-like, I fulfilled the assignments. I knew I would draw again. I had an inkling of my familiar self. Not only did I feel the liberation of making art but looked forward to analyzing it from a therapeutic point of view. I was living proof of Kramer's idea that in art therapy form and content are equally important. I knew that when I had more control of my arm and hand, I would recognize how my art would make sense of sorting out and mastering my psychological and real experiences.

As the class progressed, our project was to draw self-portraits. Easy, I thought. Now I was in familiar territory. What emerged was me in a hospital gown, looking lost and about thirteen, with a blue scarf around my neck.

In the classroom, we exchanged portraits with the person sitting across from us at the long table and then moved next to them. The woman across from me appeared to be in her late fifties. Her face sagged with lack of expression. She wasn't wearing make-up and her hair hung limply.

I wouldn't have noticed her if I hadn't been instructed to interact with her. I knew nothing about her. Her self-portrait showed a beautiful younger woman with the same blond hair and features. Her parted red lips smiled seductively, her dark eyes sparkled with amusement, a pink glow covered her cheeks. "What makes you feel so beautiful?" I asked, hoping not to be too bold. "Lounge singing," she said. "I loved singing my heart out for years in those smoky clubs, people sipping cocktails, all eyes on me. Then I stopped to take care of my mom. She's old and needs me."

"Can't you do both?" I asked.

"I have to," she said. "I've become numb inside because I stopped. Hey, maybe there really is something to this art stuff." I told her I'd love to hear her sing, and she scatted—*diddly oop bop shabam she boo be yap*—softly in my ear. When she stopped, she looked like her self-portrait.

After months in the classroom, the next phase of the training was to do an art therapy residency. Mine was at New York Hospital while still an outpatient at St. Vincent's. I was nervous but anxious not to be the one who needed fixing. The boundary blurred between the patient in the bed and me. I wore my turquoise blouse with matching scarf wrapped around my neck and long pants covering my Jobst as I sat beside her. My role was reversed a few hours each week. Adopting the lilt of my physical therapist Merry's voice as my own, I addressed my patient, "How are you feeling today, sweetie?"

"Eh, I wish I could get out of here."

"I'm going to take you on a little vacation right now. Are you ready?" I held up the crayons and paper.

"What do you mean? I can't draw a straight line. Just leave me alone. I don't feel well." She closed her eyes, clutched the cover under her chin, and turned her head away from me.

"Trust me," I said. I leaned over the bed and put my hand over hers, hoping to engage her. I waited a couple of minutes, then said, "Relax. Take a deep breath through your nose, letting it fill your belly and travel up your body to your head." She pretended I wasn't there. I rubbed her hand and softly asked her to take a deep breath again. She finally did in the form of a sigh of resignation. "Good. Take another one through your nose, this time filling your body," I repeated gently. She was with me. "Now release it and feel your body sink into the bed. Keep your eyes closed. Think of a place you've been to that you love—what it looks like, how the air feels on your skin, the smells. Are you there now? Is anyone with you?" I waited for a nod. "Okay, open your eyes but keep that picture in your mind."

I handed her the art supplies. "Now draw what it feels like to be there. It doesn't have to be a replica of the place. It can be anything you want just to give you that feeling. Use the colors you see in your mind. This is your world." She began tentatively.

"Nice," I said. The momentum built and eventually she covered the page with swirling blue shapes interspersed with little silver stars. She put down the art supplies, sighed with exhaustion. "What do you think?" she asked.

"Fantastic. Let's tape it somewhere near your bed so you can look at it. By the way, is this any particular time or place?"

She smiled and said, "It's the night I met my husband, may he rest in peace. Thank you, honey. I'm gonna get some sleep now."

I left the room having grown about an inch. The shared moment of bridging the patient to her relief made me feel strong, compassionate, and connected to her. With her thank you and smile still in my head, I forgot about my wounds.

I entered the office of an administrator to report on the session. I noticed her staring at the Jobst on my hands. "I see you've been burned," she says. "You must have been through a tremendous ordeal. I doubt if you could survive another one." She zapped me into feeling like a patient. I wanted to crawl into the nearest empty bed. Her words amplified in my head like a broadcast system in a stadium. I looked around to see if anyone had heard them.

That night I dreamt I found out about a little old lady in a cabin in a lush forest. She had just woken up from a sleep that lasted years and resembled a delicate piece of porcelain with small chiseled features and smooth white hair. Someone warned me not to go there, but I wanted to bring her food and felt I belonged in that cabin. I was informed that she didn't have teeth, so I broke up crackers and cut lox into small pieces to take to her. When I woke up, I ran to the mirror not knowing if I would see myself, my mother, or an old lady.

The image of my own face assured me I could take care of myself and extend myself to others' care.

Continuing my own physical therapy and once again painting with watercolors made me stronger.

᧑

IN THE YEAR SINCE MY ACCIDENT, I'D BECOME OBSESSED WITH THE intimate knowledge of how life can change drastically in a flash and was drawn to people who had that experience. I saw other people's flaws as the most interesting parts of their faces and bodies. Mental and physical wounds were the stuff that moved and inspired me, but I still couldn't accept them in myself. Pema Chödrön, an American Buddhist nun and author of *When Things Fall Apart*, wrote, "Nothing ever goes away until it teaches us what we need to know."

I was eager to use my new skills as an art therapist. Through Hospital Audiences, an agency that sends artists to senior centers and facilities for the mentally ill, physically disabled, and seriously sick children, I had short part-time jobs in the far reaches of all five boroughs. After hours on the subway, with a scarf wrapped around my neck and art supplies in hand, I entered an old-age home, the smell of urine and disinfectant permeating the air. Instead of heading for the nearest bathroom or the door, I focused on the brigade of sweet elderly people in wheelchairs and with walkers who smiled and squeezed my hand when I arrived. They just wanted to talk and have a new person visit them. They had neither the desire to make art nor the confidence they could. After brief conversations with each person, I pulled out the art supplies and set them on the long table in the center of the room. I cajoled everyone to join me at the table, beginning by guiding them through the visualization exercises I perfected during my student residency. They relaxed in their chairs; their faces became calm.

Rosalie, hunched over in her wheelchair, made a picture of sand with colored rectangles on it, the ocean a blue-green band of color and a horizon line with a very blue sky above and a bright yellow sun in the middle. She proudly handed it to me. "This is Rockaway Beach. I took my five kids there every summer for years. There was a designated lost and found area on the boardwalk. One of the kids usually slipped away, but I knew where to find him. Those were the days." She beamed.

Saul slumped in his chair. "No art for me today, sweetheart. Can you just hold my hand a little while? You remind me of my granddaughter. I don't remember the last time I saw her." I gently held his bony, wrinkled hand. I realized that I loved people's stories, glimpses into a world other than my own.

At the residences for adults with disabilities, I did diagnostic projects besides the therapeutic ones. Some of these residents looked like they were in their sixties but were really in their forties. They had taken medication for decades, which slowed them down, making their muscles atrophy and minds less alert. It didn't matter what I asked them to draw, the materials dictated the results. Many of them made paintings of detailed repetitive patterns, a sign of autism. Others drew wild creatures and figures rivaling any outsider art I had seen in galleries.

These experiences led to a year-long job from a grant to Babies Hospital at Columbia Presbyterian Hospital. I was part of a team that included a psychiatrist, pediatrician, psychologist, social workers, and dance therapist. As an art therapist, I occupied the lowest rung on the therapeutic ladder and was referred to as the arty scarf lady, always wearing a scarf to hide my secret. We worked with abused children from infants to six-year-olds and their mothers, who neglected them, abused them, or didn't prevent other people they knew from doing so. The court mandated the mothers participate or else they would lose their children. The team's diagnosis was that the children had severe developmental delays, some mentally handicapped. Through simple art projects, I contributed my informational piece about each family and child. I thought that perhaps this extreme trauma presented itself as delays because these children were so young and didn't have the skills to cope with what happened. Maybe I could reach them.

The sessions designed to bond the moms and kids were focused times for them to share an art activity and observe how they interacted. I cherished my time alone with the kids. Part of me identified with them being victims of circumstances beyond their control. I wanted to help minimize their trauma in the same way that the act of being their guide minimized my own.

Keisha was a four-year-old girl raped by her uncle. No one ever heard her speak. The doctors diagnosed her as mentally retarded. (This was an acceptable description in the 1980s, changed to intellectually disabled in 2013.) When I met Keisha, she looked terrified. In her I saw myself as also having been through something horrific and not having a voice to communicate the unimaginably terrible experience that had replaced a piece of myself. No one at this job knew that I always wore a scarf around my neck to hide the still blazing red scar beneath it; neither did they know about the fire that caused it.

I sat on the floor in front of Keisha. I reached for her hand. Pointing to the carpet, I asked her to join me. She sat down. I gently held her little shoulders, smiled, and put all my attention into her brown eyes. When she held my gaze, I picked up a card painted red and repeatedly said "red." Then I pointed to her shoes and red dress and said "red." I pointed to the parts of my plaid blouse that were red and repeated naming the color. She followed my gaze silently. The next time I did the same thing with a yellow card, pointing to everything in the room that was yellow.

Each session I added another color—blue card, green card, orange card, and purple card backed up by pointing to and naming the colored objects in the room. I gave her paints. I pointed to a color, named it, and asked her to make a design with it. Then I gave her another color, named it, and asked her to add it to her design. She was totally absorbed but mute. Her tongue traced her upper lip in concentration as she painted. Her eyes were alive, and she had good control of the brush.

On our sixth session, Keisha gingerly walked into the room. When she spotted me, she ran toward me with a big smile and hugged my waist. She pointed to a circle on the blue polka dot scarf around my neck. "Blue," she said. It was the first time she had uttered a word. I squeezed her tight, screaming "YES!" She pointed to the blue crayon on the table and said "blue" again. I took off my scarf and asked her if she would like it. "Yes," she said and I tied it around her waist.

At the weekly staff meeting, I recounted Keisha's progress. "The best part is she SAID blue," I announced. "My experience of that little girl has been one of a scared, traumatized child raped before she was two, not someone who is retarded." I hoped they would reconsider their diagnosis. What did I really uncover? I needed Keisha to be OK. I knew that if she moved away from her trauma by speaking, I would be able to do the same with mine as an artist and art therapist.

"She's totally different than when I met her. When she feels safe and engaged in something she likes, she expresses herself. SHE SPOKE FOR THE FIRST TIME," I emphasized to my colleagues. It was the first time since I was burned that I was confident in myself and in expressing my opinion, even if someone didn't agree. I was on the verge of discovering more about my own capabilities as an art therapist and as an advocate for people I wanted to help. As I continued my presentation, I felt my heart expanding, a physical softening in my chest. I played a part in this child taking a giant leap out of her fear. I believed that I had witnessed a miracle. Taken over by emotion, face flushed, I felt like a pile of mush in a room of impartial diagnosticians.

The psychiatrist said, "We're glad she responds to making art with you, but that doesn't mean she's not retarded. By the way, you're not wearing a scarf."

"I know," I smiled, my fingers ever so briefly caressing my neck.

6

HOME

"**D**ARLING, IT'S MARVELOUS TO SEE YOU WITH A PAINT brush in your hand, but there are blue spots on the linoleum," my mother cried when she came upstairs to the vestibule outside the gray room. The watercolors I started using splattered the floor. She complained about the mess as if I were a five-year-old instead of thirty-three.

"Ma, I'm doing a project for my art therapy class. Remember, I'm a painter? I'm learning how to use art to help people."

"But you're ruining my floor."

At this point I did most things for myself, albeit very slowly. It was finally time to move back to Tribeca. My parents drove me to my loft several times to help me get things in order. My father installed a chinning bar at the entrance to my bedroom so I could hang from it to stretch my arm. They left me at the loft for a few hours each time to make sure I could fend for myself. I sat and looked out the window at the water. I took out my paints and arranged them on my worktable. I looked at my old work. I was ready.

Encouraged by making small paintings for art therapy class, I just wanted to stay in my loft alone, protected from strangers' glances, and make large and messy paintings. I threw the paint Jackson Pollack style, swinging my arm, pushing my range of motion; mixed huge amounts of greens and purples in large containers, sweeping the canvas with my big scenic brushes. Adding linseed oil and turpentine, the colors bled into each other. I threw small amounts of white onto the canvas and watched the paint puddle and then pulled strands of the white through the puddles. I created surfaces that looked like marble, sort of resembling my skin except for the color, then painted trompe l'oeil doors or windows over the marble. Through those portals I depicted people who were in the midst of a seminal moment when anything could occur, reflecting the precariousness of life: a man with a fedora pointed his concealed hand in his suit jacket pocket at a woman who was standing in front of another man; she spread her arms out from her sides protectively shielding the person behind her.

My body screamed *wham wham*, alive with the straining of my muscles and tendons. Painting and swinging my arm, I didn't feel the loneliness until I stopped, exhausted.

When I finished a couple of these paintings, I called the dealers that previously represented my work.

"Hi, Roberto, it's Brahna. It's been a while. How are you? I have some great new paintings. I'd love you to come over and see them."

"Darling, it's been ages," he said. "We'd love to see your work. You must have a loft full of them by now. We were wondering why we haven't heard from you in over a year! We tried calling, but the recording said the line was temporarily disconnected. Are you still in Tribeca?"

"I am," I said, paused and continued. "I'm sorry that I've been out of touch. I . . . I had an accident."

Roberto jumped right in. "Oh dear. Are you all right?"

"Yes, I'm good now. I was in a fire, but I'm painting again and the paintings are strong and exciting."

"Tell me about the work. Is it like the parachute paintings or the muscle men? Is it very different from what we sold?"

"It's more narrative. Still my style. But, yes, different. I really want you to come over. You'll be blown away."

"Is it about being burned?" His voice lowered. "Honey, it must have been terrible. Tell me, are you very scarred?"

"It's not about being burned, but the experience influenced my work, of course. Don't worry about my skin." I worried enough for everyone. I wished I had the detached wonderment I felt a few years ago when I noticed a powerful hand dryer in a ladies room make the skin on the back of my hand ripple like wind does to water on a lake. I no longer looked at my skin with wonderment, knowing how much it absorbed me once I started and wanting to get past my surface.

"Darling, we are concentrating more on the secondary market now and going to Europe for a while. Would love to see your work when we return. Please take care of yourself, honey, and keep painting. Ciao."

I REMEMBERED HOW THEY CAME TO REPRESENT ME WHEN I FIRST arrived in New York. Bursting with unfettered hope, I studied *Art News, Artforum, Art in America,* and the *Soho News,* bought at Untitled, a shop on Prince Street. A small notice announced that an uptown gallery was looking at artists' slides every Wednesday. I had already made the rounds of Soho galleries and received compliments but not commitments, which dampened but didn't discourage my efforts. In the downtown hotbed of discovery, I was just another of the many hopeful black-clad young artists wanting her shot at recognition. I had face-to-face contact with the Soho power brokers like cigar-chomping Ivan Karp, who delivered the rejection personally. He softened the blow, saying, "interesting work, my dear, but it doesn't fit into the image of OK Harris. Don't be discouraged. Try other galleries," as he handed me back my slides. I was determined to have my work shown even if I had to take a circuitous route to the Mecca of SoHo.

The first Wednesday after seeing the notice my fingers clutched the handles of a small leather portfolio with a large red zipper around the edge, containing plastic slide sheets. Each little square on the eight-by-ten-inch sheet had an image of my work of the last three years. Enclosed were also photos of my paintings, reviews of exhibitions in California, and my resume. I really wanted them to show my work. *They will love it. They will love it.* I repeated as a mantra to myself on the subway.

That day, three years before my phone call with Roberto, I had emerged from the R train clad in black peg leg jeans, black leather jacket, and short black-heeled boots, my long dark hair waving like a banner. On 57th Street, I noticed that the men in suits and women in skirts with coiffed hair and matching high heels and handbags moved at a more clipped pace than my dashing long strides. The uptown formal rushed seriousness was not my scene, preferring downtown casual seriousness, like hanging out at Broome Street Bar defending my use of blended smooth surfaces of paint to the scraggly artist on the next barstool who thought paintings with heavy layers of paint applied with a palette knife were the only ones with any heft. Yet this other aspect of New York intrigued me—the impeccable attire and sense of purpose of continuously moving sophisticates along the concrete boulevard lined by windows displaying gorgeous clothes and accessories like colorful candies and pastries, even appealing for someone without a sweet tooth—Chanel, Gucci, Hammacher Schlemmer. Uptown I was a curious tourist in another city.

When I entered the hushed gallery, I heard my nervous stomach gurgle, felt my throat struggle to swallow my saliva. The worst they can say is NO, I consoled myself. But I didn't want to hear NO. I approached the receptionist and asked to speak to the director, as I had done in Soho.

"What is this in reference to?" the young woman with every blond hair in place asked.

"I've come to show him my slides."

"Just leave them with me and he'll review them." She pointed to a large stack on the side of her desk. "Did you enclose a self-addressed stamped envelope?" she asked.

"No. I'm sorry, but my phone number is on my resume. I can return to pick them up," I said in a soft staccato, my voice breaking as I looked down at the gray carpet.

"That's fine. If you don't hear from us in a week or two, please call."

"Thank you," I mumbled, rushing to the door. How could a stupid receptionist make me feel so insignificant? Without my little portfolio, I was stripped of my identity, involuntarily naked. What if they lost it or threw it out? How could I be so dumb not to bring an envelope, in which to leave everything? That snippy mannequin wasn't about to give me one. But I had no intention of giving up.

After the fire, I understood the strength of that earlier inherent determination and multiplied it to a degree I didn't know I was capable of to fully heal. For the rest of my life, I recognized that kernel of keeping a goal in mind and using the act of creating a piece or body of work to achieve it. As a woman who looked at more aggressive people and thought I didn't know how to ask for what I needed and wanted, I realized that I did in my own externally quiet but roaring inside way. Decades later, being clear about what I wanted or needed to do followed up by the act of trying gave me hope and purpose.

None of this was in my conscious mind as a young artist looking for representation. However, a few months after dropping my slides off at the uptown gallery, four of my big parachute paintings and work of three other artists crammed the gallery walls. My canvases looked like the calmness between the waves in a sea of color and strong dark lines of the other paintings. Wandering around the room was like being in a subway car during rush hour among strangers. I just wanted to get to my destination, which was the assurance that people liked my work, would buy it, or write about it. I was too agitated to enjoy the ride. Working my way through the crowd, I landed in front of my six-by-four-foot painting of my California roommate's blurry body pushing against the parachute that enveloped it. This was my only figurative work in the show, and next to it was a red dot. It sold!! Now I was enjoying myself. Checking out my other paintings, they all had red dots. Perhaps the surface serenity as an antidote to urban life attracted the patrons. In any case, paint transformed my sexual obsession, remaining inscrutable yet seductive. I felt invulnerable.

ᔛ

THREE YEARS LATER, STARTING OVER AGAIN, I REMAINED ALONE IN my loft for weeks. I craved some companionship. Jimmy, Jacques, and their friends occasionally took me to clubs. My fashion designer friend, Mira, made me a going-out dress—a short, light mint green, polished cotton number with black piping and details. It had a neckline that settled under my chin and long tapered sleeves. I wore black tights to conceal the Jobst on my scarred legs and black gloves to cover the Jobst gloves. Although the style and fabric were quite chic, I stood in contrast to the reigning downtown diva, an eighties version of Jayne Mansfield, with her bared arms and back and plunging neckline exposing her creamy voluptuous breasts. I felt totally unsexy and undesirable but lucky to go out with Jimmy and Jacques, seated at a VIP table surrounded by a group of gorgeous young men.

ᔛ

I MISSED THE NIGHTS OF NOT-SO-LONG-AGO WHEN I COOLLY STRODE into a restaurant enjoying being seen. The art world, like chess, was a game I had just started to learn. I didn't know all the maneuvers necessary to play really well, but I was an enthusiastic acolyte. One night my friend Sandy suggested we go to the Odeon, a converted art deco cafeteria, one of Tribeca's first hip restaurants. The long bar to the left of the entrance was packed. I followed Sandy as she wiggled through the crowd, checking out who was there. Dressed in our downtown black, we blended well. Sandy caught the bartender's attention. Over the din of chatter, she shouted her order: two tequila sunrises. We couldn't stand there empty handed.

She whispered to me: "It's really important to be noticed by the big guys who rule the art world in the company of one of their own."

Sandy spotted Dennis Oppenheim, a lauded conceptual artist with wild blonde hair like matted dog's fur. He was deeply involved in conversation with a mangy cohort. She sidled up to him. He gave her a sloppy kiss on the lips and put his arm around her.

"What's up, kiddo?" he said.

"This and that. So busy, sweetie, I can barely catch my breath. This is my friend Brahna. She has a show uptown."

He turned to me and gave me a hug, tottering on his bar stool.

"Looks like you could use a little food. Let me buy you dinner. Follow me," Sandy said to him.

He rose from the bar with an arm around each of us. The crowd made way as we ambled toward the restaurant on the other side of the low frosted glass partition. The scent of homemade French fries and success wafted through my nostrils. People lined up waiting for tables, but the hostess seated us immediately in a puffy red leather upholstered banquette. At the next table, Andy Warhol held court with his entourage. Andy and Dennis acknowledged each other with nods.

"I love your work, especially the land art," I told Dennis, observing him with the intensity I used with my models: dirt around the nails of solid fingers, pale skin with ruddy chiseled cheeks, perfect small straight nose, full lips, intelligent yet mischievous blue eyes meeting mine.

"Aw, that's sweet. Thanks. I love that you love it. Are you an artist too?"

I was thrilled that he had put me in the same category as himself and nodded in affirmation. I just might be qualified to dip my toes into the holy deep sea where the big fish swam. I tried to be nonchalant. Two handsome men approached. The taller one, who looked like a model with dark hair and perfect features, made beautiful line paintings and showed at Sonnebend. The other was a famous minimalist sculptor known for the massiveness of his work.

"Hey man," Dennis said. Leaning across Sandy, he shook their hands in a manly coded clasp. They squeezed into the booth next to me. I was speechless. These were the artists whose work I studied in art school. They were so good looking, and I was sitting thigh to thigh with them!

"And who are these lovely ladies?" the sculptor, whose art and demeanor made him the classic Guy, asked. Introductions were made. I knew from interviews in art magazines that both men were married. I decided not to flirt but smiled some more, not having the opportunity to say much or the wish to interrupt the men's rattling off their latest collectors and accomplishments before they got up to join the gallerist Leo Castelli at a nearby table. The sculptor discreetly slipped a napkin with his phone number on the banquet next to me as he left. I didn't care that I wasn't involved in any deep conversations. Clearly, this wasn't the place for that. What mattered was that I was there in the inner sanctum. I was meeting the legends and they thought I was the cute new arrival with dark hair shorter than theirs. I smiled. I couldn't stop smiling. I was exactly where I wanted to be.

✍

THE PHONE IN MY LOFT RANG, DISTRACTING ME FROM PAINTING. IT was my friend Wendy, my scenic painting buddy from a few years before.

"Hi, Brahna, long time no see. When are you going to start hanging out again?" she said.

"I don't know if I'm ready. Kind of busy with painting, art therapy, my own physical therapy."

"Listen, I haven't been the most attentive friend, the English boy I've been dating is taking all my time, but I don't want you turning into a nun. I have a great roommate you should meet."

"What? What kind of roommate? Why should I meet him and why would he want to meet me?"

"Because Lorenzo's hot, loves women and is perfect for you right now." I couldn't believe she was trying to set me up. I was not ready to take my Jobst and clothes off and have sex, especially with a stranger.

"He's a real sweetheart. You should see him with his son—great dad. And considerate? Whenever we run out of toilet paper, he's the one who goes to the store and brings back rolls of it."

"But is he going to be turned off by my scars?" I was turned off by my scars.

"Honey, he's a sex machine. He won't be turned off by any part of you. Think about it." That night in my sleep I wanted to masturbate. To my dismay, I woke before orgasm because I had too many of those damn scar compression garments to remove.

The next day I called Wendy and invited her and Lorenzo to come over. When I buzzed them up and the elevator opened, the only person in it was a handsome tall man with beautiful curly hair and big brown eyes that smiled as much as his lips did. He told me Wendy sent her apologies, but couldn't make it and offered to take me out for a glass of wine. I nervously rang for the elevator to return immediately, cautious about having a strange man in my loft. I relaxed more after some wine and talking about music and art, in which he was involved. It was easy to talk to him and he was gorgeous.

"I'd love to see your paintings," he said. "I caught the smallest glimpse when I came in and would really like to see more." We returned to my building. After looking at the work, he asked me to show him the rest of the loft. As if in a daze, I led him to my bedroom, the only room not in the open space. I let him pull me down on the bed. We both had all of our clothes on. He held my head in his hands and kissed me. It was the first time I had kissed a man in over a year. It was easy and spontaneous; the closeness of this man was delicious. We didn't stop kissing until I needed to take a breath. He removed the turquoise scarf from my neck. I pushed him away. I was not ready for anything else to come off. *Me encanta*," he whispered. Ooh the flattery made me limp and light-headed, thinking I might be desirable. However, the virginal sixteen-year-old I felt like at that moment didn't want to go any further and expose my unchartered body. I needed time to adjust in my mind to what my flesh wanted. I asked him to call me and he agreed.

After I didn't hear from him for a few days, I called Wendy and asked, "What do you think Lorenzo is doing right now?"

"I don't know. He's out. Why do you want to know? I thought you weren't that into him."

"Not true. I just wasn't ready to do anything else that night. Now I can't stop thinking about him. You think he'll call me?"

He did. When he stepped out of my elevator, I greeted him wearing a long silky caftan—thank you, Aunt Sylvia—without Jobst underneath. I didn't need to get naked to have sex.

"I was in a fire and have scars. I don't want you to see them," I said in between kisses, laying on my bed in the dark.

"I know," he murmured, while ardently running his hands over my covering, then working them underneath and removing my panties. About to go down on me, I didn't want him to see the donor sites on my thighs, so I gently placed my hand over his eyes. He took my hand away.

"Don't worry about your scars. You're beautiful," he said.

"You really think so?"

"Yes. Not in the same way as Marilyn Monroe, but in your own way."

That was good enough for me. It was the first time making love with a man since the fire—a landmark night. I felt like the old me again on the inside.

Yet a few days later, I began to feel sad because I doubted I had the same allure to keep a man who wanted more than just a fuck. Lorenzo opened me up to my passionate sexual self, a familiar older instinct, yet I still felt unattractive and deformed in my new body. He came over the next week, and we made love fueled by the sweet nothings he constantly whispered. I wanted to make plans to go out and do things together.

"This isn't the time for you to have a boyfriend," he said. "You have to take care of yourself." I didn't hear from him often, but he was the first step in seeing myself as not repulsive. He opened the possibility for intimacy.

He was right about taking care of myself. Scheduled for another round of skin grafts, on the gurney, waiting for them to wheel me into the operating room, I was desperately alone in the endless gray halls, cold underneath a thin white cotton blanket.

When Dr. Haher came to the hospital room the next day, she told me that my arm would never look the same as before, but there was tremendous improvement. Somehow, this time it registered. My right arm would never look like my left arm, and I started losing hope of looking "normal," of ever wanting to expose my mangled limb. I would never wear a sleeveless blouse or workout top in public. I kept my arms covered but came to realize that it was a small voluntary price in exchange for having the use of my arm. However, in that moment in the hospital bed, I was devastated to learn that regardless of the surgeries and therapy to improve the motion, the massive scarring would always be there. Immersed in self-pity, I didn't hear the part about the improvement or see how much I was ruled by vanity.

I exhausted myself in outpatient therapies and painting. I slept deeply. In my dreams, my skin was perfect. When I woke I sensed that inside my charred body lived a voluptuous sensual woman of goddess stature. However, shortly afterward, looking at my skin, waves of negativity knocked me down. Because I saw myself as appearing damaged, I accepted any crumb of physical attention as a gift, as if lying under a tree looking up toward the sun hoping for a few rays to find me hidden in the shadows. I spent much time alone, maybe too much.

Breaking my isolation, the bell rang from downstairs. Thinking it was food delivery, I buzzed him up. When the elevator door opened, I was surprised to see Bob the sculptor from across the street. Before the fire, I often saw him outside his building chiseling large pieces of stone. In warm weather, he worked bare chested, his sexy exposed torso a beacon for my desire, then. Before the fire, we had casual sex but were not close friends.

"Oh, I thought you were Fresh Direct," I said.

"I could be," he answered, holding a casserole dish in his hand. "But seriously, it's so good to see you." He looked concerned and gave me a friendly hug. "I was so freaked out the day I saw you carried into the ambulance. After all this time, I noticed you open your front door the other day and just had to see how you're doing," he said.

"Wow, how nice of you," I said, for the first time seeing him as a kind neighbor.

"Here's some lasagna. I'm married now, and my wife's a great cook. When I told her what happened to you, she insisted I bring this." I never realized what a real, caring person he was. I had just seen him as a stallion, and I had not been interested in knowing more about Bob at that time. His presence made me realize that before the fire I was attracted to men for their sexual appeal and their artistic achievement. Now that I no longer saw myself as physically desirable, I was horrified at how superficial I had been. I had objectified men in the same way they did women.

My neighbor's thoughtfulness and humanity made me see what I had missed by just looking at him on the surface. What else had I missed through the narrow lens of my past self-involvement? My current self-involvement was self-pity. I hoped this was a temporary painful stop on the path of change.

My emotions were a tangle of contradictions. At the sporadic times Lorenzo called, I was always available, knowing it would never be a relationship. It was on his terms, but having him as a lover was better than not having one. Damaged burn victims can't be choosy, I thought. My body wanted him. His sweet nothings really were nothing. I had shifted from dependent child to hormone-driven teenager in my developmental rebirth. Making love was as exceptional as it was at nineteen when I grew attached to my first lover because he was my first lover, an indelible presence. I now spent my time being "the art lady" as an art therapist, painting in my loft and waiting for the phone to ring.

∽

I RETURNED HOME FROM MY ART THERAPY JOB EAGER TO TAKE OFF my clothes reeking of the smell of Lysol. As I stripped down to just the confinement of my Jobst, I noted the blinking light of the answering machine and pushed "listen," hoping it would be Lorenzo.

"This is a blast from your past. It's Kevin. I'm living in New York City now, trading on Wall Street. Looked you up in the phone book and thought I'd say hi. Call me."

The familiarity of his voice made me dizzy. I sat down and listened again, feeling an inner nervous jiggle. As if in a daze, I wrote down the number. I hadn't seen him in over a decade.

∽

KEVIN WAS MY FIRST LOVER, MY MAIN BOYFRIEND FROM 1968–1972—ten years my senior, stockbroker, graduate of Notre Dame, a "fighting Irish" football player with an MBA. It was clear to me, his Jewish flower child girlfriend, that Kevin prided himself in being successful in the straight business world while having close encounters with the San Francisco hippie counterculture through me. For four years, he tempted me with one adventure after another by providing the kind of fun and sophistication that boys of my age and generation couldn't.

We drove his VW bug to San Blas and Mazatlan at Christmas. It was the first time I entered a Catholic Church redolent with gold figures of Jesus, Mary, and Saints. Kevin took my hand, and we joined the line of people waiting to approach the alter. I thought the priest placing a cracker on each awaiting tongue was a Christmas treat. As we approached, Kevin told me I would be swallowing the body of Christ. I bolted for the streets where people were singing and dancing, and my boyfriend joined me after his sacrament.

We rode his motorcycle up the winding roads of Mount Tamalpais—named "the sleeping lady" by the Indians for its silhouette—the eucalyptus-scented air whipping our faces. As we descended the curves of the mountain leading to the natural untamed beach community of Bolinas, I felt the freedom and beauty echoed by the quixotic weather on that side of the mountain. The fog could roll in at any moment, changing the warm summer sun into a misty chilly day, then be replaced by a sunny autumn wind, turning back to a warm still sunset.

Kevin's sprawling redwood weekend house on a rise above the water was an isolated hide-a-way where nothing existed but views and the prospect of pleasure. However, the clash of his aggressive personality with submissiveness and idealism often led to squabbling. We both had strong opinions, but often my timidity prevented me from expressing mine. At nineteen, although passionate about everything, my identity as a woman and artist was tenuous. In a way, I was like a firmly rooted reed that easily moved with every breeze. Kevin always created a strong wind. My only retaliation was to point out the difference between the worlds we inhabited when we weren't together. I emphasized that regardless of how cool he thought he was, he was still very much a part of the "establishment." Being part of the generation that wanted to change the values of our society, I felt I could contribute this through my art. While we were melting wax in pots on the stove to make candles, he said, "You think being an artist is a laid-back profession, and you can enlighten the world. I think artists are egotists. Look at those guys doing land art. They have the balls to change nature. That's so much more aggressive than what I do."

"They aren't changing nature," I argued defensively. "They are making a statement about humans and the environment. They use the landscape to create site-specific sculptures that are not permanent alterations."

"Well, I like those big stretches of land in the middle of nowhere left pristine," he said. Looking back, I realize that all our arguments were about male artists compared to him. My art, because I was a woman, was of no consequence to Kevin unless it had to do with his ego or pleasure. Blindly, I let that define me when I was with him.

"You're just jealous of their creativity."

"Let me show you how creative I am," he said, picking me up and carrying me to the bedroom. Lightheaded after passionate lovemaking, we went to the beach, walking on the soft fine sand nestled below rock cliffs of the same color. Pine cones and coral bumped up against each other. The overflow of lush vegetation capping the cliffs spiraled down. We picked up pitted and striated rocks, stopping to make little altars and sculptures along the beach that others would change with their additions. We played in the cold ocean, splashing each other like children, then warmed up snuggling on our beach blanket, legs entwined.

Upon returning, the house was ablaze, surrounded by fire engines. Only then did I remember the wax on the stove. I looked at Kevin and the crumbling rental home.

"There go my Brooks Brothers suits," he said.

How unfathomable that twelve years later, I would be ablaze.

After the Bolinas fire, Kevin left his job at the brokerage firm. Always the shrewd businessman, he decided to import clothing and jewelry from Indonesia. Demand was on his side.

We arranged to meet in Greece as soon as I received my bachelor's degree in sociology and jewelry design. The money to travel was a graduation gift from my parents. Being free to explore the world had been my mother's dream had she not married so young. It was a generous gift with the understanding that after I had seen Europe for a couple of months, I would come home, settle down, maybe with Kevin or better yet someone who was Jewish, and start a regular life putting my education to use.

But when I arrived in Athens, Kevin was not at our designated meeting place—a little taverna steps from the Acropolis. I took a simple room above the restaurant for $1 a night. I had traveled abroad alone once before, and since I expected Kevin to show up at any moment, it felt like the beginning of a new adventure. After a week of exploring the city, I traveled to Istanbul.

When I returned to Athens, about to go back to the States and visit my parents, I stopped at communication central—the American Express office—and found a letter from Kevin. He apologized and wanted to see me. I was still in love him. For me, his charisma lay in his daring, quick intelligence and good looks that combined a broad smile and athleticism, recalling a renegade version of JFK. He was what I wanted at the time.

I agreed to see him. When we met he said, "Wow, baby, you look far out. I'm so sorry I messed up. Lost track of time in the caves in Matala. I don't want to lose you and never meant to hurt you. Please let me make it up to you. I want to travel with you. My treat."

"I don't know. I told my parents I was coming home," I said.

"Tell them you're extending your trip. I have friends who will drop us at a remote cove on a beach in Mykonos. We can stay there for a few weeks, then Crete for a few weeks, then Beirut. Doesn't that sound better than Brooklyn?"

His confidence, ability to take charge—especially in sticky

situations—and the promise of love, adventure, and traveling with a protective lover hooked me.

In 1970 Beirut was the Paris of the Middle East and not on the well-trodden route for young American travelers. We sat in cafes looking at the pastel buildings of the city washed in light. I felt very sophisticated at twenty-one, like a heroine in one of the French New Wave films I had devoured just five years earlier at the Bleecker Street cinema.

One night someone we met at the hotel took us to the outskirts of town. On a dirt lot with blades of grass here and there, we entered a Bedouin home constructed of newspaper and mud, topped with a tin roof. Three generations of men sat in a circle on the floor playing music with hand-held drums. The women, whose faces were tattooed, took turns belly dancing in the center to the men's drumbeat and the tinkling of their own brass finger cymbals. When the oldest woman entered the center of the circle, she beckoned me to join her. She appeared to be in her seventies, though it was hard to determine her age since her body was swathed in fabric and her face and hands covered with tattoos. I danced toward her and received my first belly dance lesson from the matriarch of the clan. My freestyle hippie bump and grind transformed into a new rhythm that focused on my hips and stomach. The enthusiastic crowd let out guttural yelps, their tongues tickling the roofs of their mouths in a particular way. I had found my primordial Semitic roots and felt oddly at home.

"I'm glad you had a great time with our new friends," Kevin said the next day. "Today we are going to visit their relatives in a small mountain village." We drove for hours, following a crude hand-drawn map that passed through the lush fragrant cedars of Lebanon.

We finally reached an isolated shack surrounded by acres of barren land where a family of seven greeted us. One son, Ahmed, who was in his twenties, spoke broken English, while everyone else spoke Arabic. It was not a belly-dancing crowd. They raised chickens.

"Why did we come here instead of staying in the beautiful cypress forest?" I asked Kevin. I was car sick and confused.

"We're only staying a few days. It's a business side trip," he said, which led me to assume the women made clothes or jewelry.

In the late afternoon of the third day, Kevin's eyes sparkled with excitement. The sun had merged his freckled skin into an overall tan and made his red hair strawberry blond and his blue eyes bluer. He told me we were going to Damascus the next day, another adventure.

We immediately hit the Syrian markets, which surpassed any I had ever seen. We bought chests and tables inlaid with mother of pearl, wool rugs in vibrant reds and oranges and sewn together like a patchwork quilt. I stroked the embroidered black satin bolero jackets, multicolored velvet and cotton long dresses with embroidered panels, and striped silk coats. They were soft and moved gracefully on my body as I twirled around the hotel room trying them on. I felt like a Middle Eastern princess in her finery fingering the silver necklaces, bracelets, rings with carnelian, and beautiful brass vessels that looked like glowing pig snouts. We loaded six huge plywood crates with the spoils of our frenzied shopping sprees. Pointing to one of the boxes, filled with the objects I had chosen, Kevin said, "This is my present to you."

He shipped the crates to California. About a month later, the treasures arrived in San Francisco. Kevin rented a truck and we took them to his big house tucked in the woods of northern Marin County.

I could hardly wait to see all the beautiful treasures. I grabbed a hammer and started prying loose the plywood box.

"Careful," Kevin shouted.

At that moment, there was a knock on the door. Kevin looked out the window and told me to go into the bedroom. Before I could protest, two men with shades, dusty motorcycle jackets, and boots stomped into the room.

"Hey, man, I see the boxes finally got here," said the one with dark greasy long-hair and tattoos. "Yeah," Kevin replied. "Can you come back in an hour after I unpack? Everything's cool."

Noting my frozen pose, the other man said, "We'll hang outside for a while."

About to ask what was happening, I noticed the middle layer of the plywood was crumbling. It had the familiar sweetish odor of hashish. I walked toward it.

"Step back. Don't touch the box," Kevin said, his freckles obliterated by the redness taking over his cheeks, a sure sign of his distress. In that moment the reality of the situation hit me. Sheets of hashish formed the middle layer of the sides of the box.

"Kevin, you're unbelievable!! You used me," I shouted. "I always knew you had perfected the art of bullshit, but you've really outdone yourself, taking me on a drug smuggling scam as your front to make you look like a tourist or legitimate businessman!!" I could hardly catch my breath. The gravity of the situation caused me to lose my ingenious self. When he had stood me up in Athens, it was hurtful, but I was still in control of my life and truly thought I was done with him. In this moment, I not only hated him but also hated myself for being so willing to be blindly trusting.

"You were never my excuse. I couldn't let you know. If by some chance I got caught, I didn't want you to be involved. I thought you would dig the adventures we had and the beautiful things I bought for you. I wanted you to be with me to share these incredible experiences because I love you. That part of the world is changing so fast. You've got to dig that," he said.

He went over to kiss me, but I pushed him away as I screamed, "Love? You didn't bring me along out of love!"

"I didn't tell you about the hash because I was protecting you. I would never do anything to hurt you. There was a whole lot more pleasure than business in this trip, wouldn't you agree? I loved having you with me. But I sell whatever brings me the highest profit. That's what I do."

I just stared at him. His pride in his cunning produced bile in my stomach, and I thought I would vomit. My lover was a drug smuggler. He had more than proven he was no longer a member of "the establishment." Could he possibly believe I thought this was cool? Yes, I was part of the generation that wanted to change the rules, but Kevin's road was a dead end. I hadn't let myself see the truth, wrapped up in my passion for him and the excitement of travel. I had refused to see the obvious until there was nowhere else to look.

Kevin carefully took the boxes apart. I didn't want any of the contents. I left the lamp, the clothes, the furniture, the jewelry, and the boyfriend behind.

༄

TRADING ON WALL STREET. HOW PERFECT, I THOUGHT, revitalizing my memory of him. Did I really want to speak to him again? After deliberating a while, I decided yes I wanted a connection to my past, to a time when I felt desired. Looking back, I realized that because of his brashness and deceptions, I always knew I would never be with him forever; I would never feel like he was family. When he answered the phone, my breath quickened, a little electric current shot through my body. I felt my face grow hot and grinned involuntarily. For a moment, I felt young and beautiful.

"Hi, Kevin. What a surprise to hear from you."

"Babe, I'd know that voice anywhere. You little fox. I'm so glad you called back. Did you see my picture on the cover of *Newsweek*?"

"No, I missed it. What was that about?"

"They did a huge article on trading futures. I was one of a bunch of guys standing in the pit of the Stock Exchange screaming. That's what I'm into. Pork bellies, soy beans whatever."

I had no idea what he was talking about, but it sounded fairly disgusting. If anyone could sell something that didn't exist yet, he could. I was no longer impressed at how easily he moved through the world, grabbing the financial gain he took as his entitlement. Same old self-satisfied braggart, I thought, feeling distanced and in control. However, my vanity kicked in, glad that he needed to impress me. "I really want to see you," he continued. "Catch up. Take you out to Lutece, unless you're married to a jealous guy. What have you been up to?"

It was sort of fun playing on the phone.

"Well, since I saw you," I started slowly, not sure what to reveal first. "I've had a burgeoning art career. Been too busy to marry."

"So I still have a chance?" He said with a strained chuckle.

"Sweet . . . there's something you need to know," I said slowly. "The most recent thing that happened was that I almost died."

"What? Are you OK, honey? Were you in a car accident?"

"No. A fire. But I'm doing really well . . . "

"Fire? Like you were burned?"

"I'm fine now and can tell you as much as you want to hear when we go to Lutece. It's quite a story." I couldn't help myself from wanting to see where this would lead.

"And I really want to hear it." He cleared his throat. I wanted to say "sure you do," but I let a beat go by. "When can I see you?" he said. "Let me call you back," I said, rubbing by my thin, itchy skin under the Jobst.

7

REBUILD

I HAD CLOSED THE KEVIN PORTION OF MY LIFE, BUT OUR phone encounter reminded me of my prior attractive self and put California on my mind. I still couldn't reconcile the appearance of my body with who I was inside. I thought someone could fix me. Richard Pryor, the comedian, severely burned by freebasing in 1980, was damaged by fire as I had been. Because he was a celebrity, he had access to the best reconstructive surgeon in Los Angeles, touted by the papers as a miracle worker. I decided to go to California to consult with his doctor. After four years, I revisited the place where I had first felt comfortable in my own skin. Now that skin no longer resembled who I had been. Catching my reflection in the mirror in the ladies' room at LAX, I wondered if my friends would recognize this woman whom I hardly knew.

Phil and Nancy greeted me at the luggage carousel with their blonde, American movie star good looks and big toothy smiles. Their gentle hugs squeezed out a deep breath of relief at their familiarity and coolness about not mentioning any changes they observed with their keen artists' eyes.

They drove me to see Dr. G., Richard Pryor's surgeon, the next day. The surgeon spent fifteen minutes telling me what a great job Dr. Haher had done.

"Isn't there something else you can do? I don't want to look like this," I pleaded.

"Our vanity never leaves us," he said. "Just be patient. You are in Dr. Haher's good hands." Despite my disappointment of no miracle surgery, I was again enthralled with California. I left Hollywood's manicured lawns and palm trees and traveled north. Wandering alone in Sausalito, I noticed that every place in town that had played a pivotal role in my life was gone. There was nothing physically left of the past—not my body, not buildings, not my houseboat, not a lingering romance. I was impatient for the future to come when the scars would fade not only on my surface but in the way I saw myself.

Inhaling the pockets of eucalyptus in Marin, northern California crept back into me. My eyes absorbed the dark greens of wooded roads, the tree trunks covered in velvety moss, which up close looked like a man's curly chest hair only emerald green, the gray-green mist, and the bright green rolling hills of Petaluma where I visited Karen at her rambling farmhouse updated with a hot tub. She stared at me as I sat stiffly, shifting in vain to feel comfortable on her horse-hair-stuffed, antique, dark red velvet sofa.

"Are you painting again?" she asked. I nodded and opened my mouth to tell her about the new work. Before the words came out, she asked, "Has being a burn victim influenced your paintings?"

My mouth still open, stunned by what I perceived as her insensitivity, I discretely put my hand under my chin to push it closed. It was the first time a friend had called me that dreaded label. Closing my eyes to squeeze away tears, I told her that while in the hospital, I realized I needed to make a film of that day. After a few moments of strained silence, Karen dialed her friend Jane Weiner, a documentary filmmaker in New York City. She briefly explained my situation, introduced me, and handed me the phone.

Across the three thousand miles I had just traveled, Jane told me she was writing a grant for a documentary on fire fighters in New York City. She wanted to interview me in her film as a burn victim saved by firemen. She said it would add strength to her grant proposal. There was that term again flashing like a neon sign in my head.

"I want to make my own film from my point of view," I said. I surprised myself by being so direct with a stranger. Was there a way to work with this person, let alone have a phone conversation with someone who called me a burn victim and wanted to interview me as one? Seen through that lens, especially twice in one day, felt like repeatedly being punched in the stomach while making an effort to stand. Why label me a victim when I survived? What about fire survivor? There is strength in that.

"I think I can work with that," she said, to my surprise. "What about you making your film within the larger context of my documentary?" she asked. I liked her quick and flexible mind. I relaxed a bit into the cushion on the sofa, feeling a sense of hope.

"Can you film me directing the recreation of that day? I need to have it as a piece of art in the world to replace its importance as the most tragic day in my life," I said, and she agreed.

"However, I don't know anything about making a film," I confessed, almost in a whisper.

"When you're back in New York, let's meet and we'll figure this out," she said. We exchanged numbers. I never expected to find this trajectory from a spontaneous phone call in cow country. What an incentive to go back home – the beginning of a new road.

∽

THE ROAD TO MAKING A FILM WOULD BE POSTPONED FOR A WHILE. Still wrapped in scar compression garments with a year of outpatient therapy under my Jobst, Dr. Haher said, "Go to the Hamptons for the summer, and let the beach heal you. I grew up spending my summers out east. It's the best cure for you right now. Swim every day in the late afternoon, and start living in the world."

In some ways, I had become comfortable in my isolation, far from my pre-fire life. After the fire, I just wanted to be invisible. My scar compression encasement became my safe house. I felt trepidation about leaving my isolation and the support system of my family. But Dr. Haher had been right about everything so far.

My mother, who placed great importance on dressing appropriately for every occasion, took me on a shopping expedition to Agnes B. and my other favorite Soho boutiques. The months in the hospital and at her house had brought us closer, and it seemed natural to follow her plan reminiscent of us shopping for clothes when I was off to college at sixteen. I needed light-weight, long sleeve cotton tops, skirts, and pants for my upcoming summer adventure.

I drove out with my parents, sitting in the back seat, more like a child being driven to summer camp than a thirty-four-year-old woman looking for her first summer rental house. I had never been to the Hamptons, which sounded so glamorous. I was the opposite of glamorous. Frozen with fear, sitting in the back of their station wagon, I wanted a life outside the structure of going to the hospital, but spending two months out east alone was a big step for someone who didn't want anyone to see her. I passed the two hours in the car cruising along the Long Island Expressway remembering family trips when I was a kid with Jimmy. With my dad at the wheel, the view of the back of my parents' heads was the same.

We pulled up to a real estate agency, and a broker drove us around until we found a small two bedroom, funky house in Amagansett on a sandy road named Treasure Island, near the ocean. This was where my new life would begin. I sublet my Tribeca loft for the price of the cottage rental.

A few weeks later, my parents moved me in with a collapsible bicycle as my only transportation. As we unloaded the station wagon, a woman opened her door across the street. Her mouth formed the shape of a perfect O as she watched my parents and me, full Jobst showing on my arm and cap on my head. When she caught my eye, she quickly changed the shape of her mouth to a smile and waved. I waved back and scurried inside. As soon as my parents left, I felt defenseless. Where the hell am I? I thought. How far can I go on that three-speed bike? I don't know anyone out here. I felt a clenching in my stomach, and my throat gulped trying to swallow. Although I had thought I was prepared to be alone, now surrounded by houses and people I perceived to be cool, I felt too self-conscious to be able to interact with them. Was I crazy thinking I could be happy plunking myself down in the midst of paradise while being too afraid to enter it?

I put on a sunhat and loose caftan, my invisibility cloak, to cover the Jobst and hurried down the block to the ocean. The waves were louder than my thoughts. The sparkles of light on the water created rainbows behind my eye lids. I walked along the edge of the water, its coolness tickling my feet. My footprints made a pattern in the wet sand, and the water instantly washed them away. Calmed by the rhythm of the sea and my walk, I headed back to the cottage. I set out my pads, pastels, oils, and pre-stretched small canvases in the living room.

∽

ON FOURTH OF JULY WEEKEND, MY FRIENDS IRENE AND SANDY drove out. I always had fun hanging out with them in the city—pre-fire. Although I hadn't socialized much since the fire, I wanted to open some of my borders, not quite knowing which ones or how much. Duplicating our past comradery would be a great way to launch my summer at the beach. As beautiful as the starry skies were my first week, the quiet was deafening. I wanted their company, and they wanted to be in the Hamptons. Anxious for action, they dragged me out dancing after they cooked dinner. While they danced and flirted, I stood on the sidelines realizing that I wasn't ready to hop onto the dance floor. I had to redefine my idea of fun and this wasn't it. I was hot and itchy but why should I expect them to want to leave? So I waited until they suggested it.

Having this house attracted phone calls from city friends I hadn't heard from in a while, all with a renewed interest in how I was faring and wanting to see me. Unlike other people who came to the East End to party, I was on a mostly monastic healing retreat in a natural paradise, not a social one. Damaged, my main purpose was repair, an opportunity to read, think, make art, become stronger.

∽

RIDING MY BIKE ALONG THE SIDEWALK ON MAIN STREET IN Amagansett, I noticed two tennis courts. A man in his early twenties patiently taught the game to kids in white shorts and tees. Tennis was never my sport, but I had an old wooden Pablo Gonzales tennis racket from sleep-away camp when I was nine. My dad insisted I bring it with me because "everyone plays tennis in the Hamptons." I dismounted my bike, walking it over the lawn, and approached the courts in my long pants and long sleeve polo.

"Can I help you?" the man asked when he called a break for the hard swinging boys.

"I'm interested in tennis lessons. Looks like you're the pro," I said, clutching onto my bike's handle bars and looking down at my gloved hands."

"Yep," he said, tilting his head to catch my averted eyes.

"I'm not very good. Actually I have a hard time even swinging a racket,"' I mumbled. "But I want to learn."

"Great. I would love to teach you," he said. I met his glance and smiled with relief instead of embarrassment.

"Should I come every day?" I asked, thinking about my old physical therapy schedule.

"How about three times a week? Maybe early morning would be best," he said, eyeing my long sleeves. "Before the heat starts up."

The next morning I biked over, my wooden racket on the clamp behind my seat.

"The last time I saw a racket like this I was five," he said. "I want you to be able to swing your arm, not have it weighed down. Wait a sec. I'll get you one of my old aluminum rackets to practice with."

After forty-five minutes of running around trying to hit the ball, I was drenched and exhausted, but I loved it. The few times I heard the ping of the ball against the racket made me want more. I was determined to be able to volley, at the least. Now I was a person who took tennis lessons like other people did.

After tennis, I biked down the block to the Amagansett Farmers' Market. Iced coffee and croissant in hand, I stepped outside to sit on a wooden bench under a tree overlooking the vast rows of flowers cultivated for cutting. Inhaling the warm and scented air, I savored every earned sip of the iced drink. After a week or so of this schedule, I self-identified as a bona fide summer resident.

Arriving home loose and sweaty, I could cool off in my outdoor shower surrounded by green and fresh smells, but I chose the one in my dark bathroom where I didn't have to look at my skin.

I rested and read Lillian Hellman, Ernest Hemingway, and books about people who lived with physical deformities. I recognized myself in Lillian Hellman's description in *Pentamento* of "an intelligent girl, flirtatious, good mannered with that kind of outward early-learned passive quality that in a woman so often hides anger." On the back deck in my Jobst, I made pastel drawings of the dunes as a way of capturing the Amagansett light.

With the passing of a few weeks, I felt a solitary pleasure after the initial shock of waking to find myself alone in the little rented cottage in a town where I didn't know anyone and was too self-conscious of my beige elastic compression garments to make friends. I slunk down the block to the roaring ocean. Without my Jobst leggings under my clothes, I rolled up my pants mid-thigh and entered the sea. The clean salty air, clear cold water, the rhythmic low thundering of the waves overtook my sensate body, feeling prickly pleasure just standing there curling my toes in the wet sand. I felt the sheer joy of life, the peacefulness of nature. This was a teaser for the afternoon swim beginning at 4:00 p.m.

✍

JIMMY AND JACQUES CAME TO VISIT. I BUBBLED WITH ANTICIPATION of spending time with my two favorite people: the fun members of my support team since the accident. I filled vases with wildflowers I picked and placed them around the guest room, contentedly making every effort for their comfort, ready to pamper them. I researched "places of interest" on the map, ones I couldn't bike to and thought they might like to share some new adventures with me.

After they settled in, relaxing on the patio with wine and cheese, I suggested we go to Montauk and buy fresh-caught fish for the weekend, showing them the little hibachi I didn't dare light. I intended to do all preparation except strike the match. I thought they would be delighted.

"Hey, we came here to relax. I've had a really busy week being at my clients' beck and call," Jimmy said. "Did you forget how hot and stinky the city is in summer? I didn't come here to be your chauffeur."

Feeling like he slammed me against a wall, I could no longer be the passive girl. The resentment of still being dependent on others and not living the full life I wanted raged inside me.

"You of all people know what I've been through. You actually saw them cut my dead skin off. I feel really lucky because I'm alive and have this little house. But it's not easy," I blubbered hysterically. I pointed to my Jobst, sweat running down my face. I didn't mean to play the victim card, but his harshness made me feel disoriented, wondering if it took only the most dire circumstances for them to care about me.

"Stop feeling sorry for yourself. If I was you . . . "

"But you're not me," I said, tears dripping into my mouth.

I ran into my bedroom. He was the beautiful golden boy with a great career, friends, and lover. No one could imagine what it was like to be me, I thought. I heard footsteps approaching my door. They halted, replaced by an accented whisper.

"Jimmy, this isn't going to work out. Let's call Ingrid and see if we can stay there. She's fabulous and knows everyone."

A few minutes later, I heard the car trunk open and close. I went outside as Jimmy approached the house.

"I don't want to fight with you. You're my sister, and I love you, but honestly, we didn't drive out here to be on your schedule. We really want to hang out at the beach and not feel responsible for you. We're going to stay with Ingrid. It's for the best."

I was stunned, crushed, and unable to respond. Having wanted the same relationship that summer weekend as when they had heroically aided my utter helplessness just a few months before, my expectations were unreasonable. I realized after the fact that they had had enough of that role; they had given all they could and wanted a weekend free of obligations. I should have gotten past being dependent, but I still was, in lesser ways. They didn't understand or care that I continued to be very vulnerable, desperate for their company and love without wanting to hamper their good time. Trying to be independent was an enormous effort, and I still needed propping up. For me, the main change in my situation was only my longitude and latitude. They had no sympathy for my isolation in paradise; they just saw the paradise. The harsh reality made me re-examine my helplessness. I couldn't have expectations of my brother fixing that. I had taken the first leap of independence and had to continue on that course. Fear of the unknown and change, even though it was wonderful change, was overwhelming.

⁓

I COULD EASILY GO BACK IN MY ROOM AND CONTINUE CRYING OR do the one thing I knew would take me out of my head: go swimming as I did every day at 4:00 p.m. Dressed in a long-sleeve, pink-and-green-striped cotton leotard and long pants to protect my raw skin from the sun, I rode my collapsible white bike three miles until I saw the expanse of the blue bay at Devon Beach.

Dismounting, I took my folded bamboo mat, towel, and book to a spot in the center of the almost deserted beach. At 4:30, the sun was still high but more muted, not the blinding light of mid-day—a winding-down light, mellow, mature, steady, not having to blast its presence; an embracing light, not a scorching one.

I virtually had the bay to myself. Submerged in the water, I licked the salt off my upper lip. Each breath took in the sight of the shore, establishing a sense of security. Only in the water did I feel whole. I had to swim to feel good and had to swim long enough to get lost in the sheer pleasure of moving. My mind no longer clung to negative thoughts. It occasionally turned to concocting opportunities in my life that seemed logical while buoyant and much more complicated when I dried off. My body spiraled, flipping over and doing the backstroke, watching the sky. As I swam, the water seeped into my long sleeves like weights wrapped around my arms. It was a challenge to keep moving, but one I enjoyed and was determined to meet.

Lost in the timeless zone of stroking, my arms and legs rhythmically hit the water, propelling me further. I alternated between the crawl and the sidestroke—for most people a relaxing movement. For me the intense forward thrust of my right arm targeted the contracting scar bands. With my head above the water, leaning on my shoulder, I gazed at the vastness of the bay and the openness of space, reflecting limitless possibilities for growth. I felt my constrictive scars loosening, my body lengthening, strengthening, elongating, emerging from the wounds, evolving into something else.

My body's impact and motion created a tune in my ears that continued as long as I kept moving. I knew at that moment this would become a practiced ritual for the rest of my life, keeping me flexible. I was chartering my own new territory.

I swam past my spot on the sand and up to the Devon Yacht Club, signaled by the moorings in the water. White wooden tables, blue canvas chairs, and blue umbrellas covered the Club's white deck. For a moment, I wanted to belong. I wanted to be a blonde with a golden tan in a bikini sitting on a deck chair with a group of friends chatting over drinks. However, I was dark haired in a long sleeve leotard, my thighs forever white—the donor sites to patch the skin on other parts of my body. The yacht club fantasy lasted about a minute, replaced by the satisfying exhaustion of my long swim and pleasure of swimming back to the beach.

I wrapped my towel around my waist to cover my vulnerable thighs and rushed my thin white pants on as soon as I dried off, not wanting to expose my legs to the sun or gaze of any passerby. Laying on the beach mat, I watched ripples of water crash on the shore, noticing how the tide had changed from when I began my swim. Green and red seaweed, pieces of wood, pebbles, and shell shards decorated the demarcation of wet sand from where the water had further receded. It was that magical time of day when everyone's skin, including mine, had that soft golden glow. The blue sky at the horizon turned purple, then pink, then light blue. The setting sun cast my purple shadow on the sand. I read a book until the sun was low over the horizon but still light enough to bike home. During the year and a half of recovery, my body had lost its normal shape, made worse by the ice cream I ate as comfort food. With all the summer exercise, my loose clothes became baggier. I swam every day for two months. My body, no longer as much of a burden, changed from stiff to fluid, from something alien to myself to becoming my vehicle as a swimmer.

I read Carl Jung and Greek mythology, fascinated by the tale of Aphrodite who was born from the sea, having been fertilized by the genitals of Uranus that had been severed and thrown into the water—the element in which I felt most alive.

At night, after the heat subsided, I set up spot lights, put my cassettes in my boom box flooding the cottage with the sounds of Brian Eno, Laurie Anderson, and Brian Ferry. I worked in a combination of pastels and oils on self-portraits from the pictures Merry took of me in physical therapy. I depicted the skin on the canvases in pastels without spraying them with fixative, permitting their image to change and blur a bit, as the scars would do over time. I saw my art and me as works in progress, noting the irony of vacationing at the beach while painting myself in a hospital gown, my eyes resembling those of a trapped animal. Yet the work marked and aided my healing. In positive moments, I slowly began to accept the change in my physical appearance.

8

THE PRINCE IN POLYESTER

I WANTED SOMEONE TO HANG OUT WITH AND INVITED Sandy to drive out alone for a weekend. My old Tribeca guide proved to be a trusty Hamptons one as well. She suggested we go to the Laundry, an East Hampton restaurant that had a lively bar scene. For the occasion, I removed my Jobst and wore a white, long-sleeved cotton jumpsuit with a jaunty silk scarf around my neck to cover the scars beneath it.

As we waited at the bar for our table, I noticed we were indisputably the youngest women in the room, and the only brunettes in a sea of blondes.

"There's Pele," Sandy whispered, tossing her head in the direction of the soccer player. I followed her gaze past the athlete and met one of a handsome man sporting an ascot. He introduced himself, adding that he played polo. Having never met a polo player before, I felt like I was in someone else's life, and it was fun. Sitting on our stools, sipping drinks, men surrounded us, introducing themselves along with revealing their professions. I guessed my camouflage was working. By the time we were led to our table, my pockets were bulging with cards from a judge, lawyers, doctors, film people—all at least ten years older than us. I was amazed that any man found me attractive. "Do you believe this?" I said to my friend.

"Don't bother to call them. They won't be able to handle your scars," she said. Although deflated deep down, I agreed with her. I was too vulnerable to take that step.

The waitress seated us at a table next to two tanned men. When they saw us, the bald one with blue eyes raised an eyebrow to his friend with a full head of dark hair and a beaked nose, who gave him a slight nod. They continued talking to each other about some kind of training schedule. I didn't know what they were referring to and wasn't listening, although there was barely a crack of separation between our tables. I was overwhelmed by the attention I had received and eating exquisitely fried calamari in a room of white table cloths, clinking glasses and silverware, animated chatter and good-looking people. I was caught in the dizzying elation blending into the crowd. Sandy, however, was listening.

"We shouldn't stay out too late. We have a busy day tomorrow—running, tennis, and swimming," she said to me in a louder than necessary voice.

I thought about the next day's line up. We might take a walk, hit some tennis balls fed to us by a Prince ball machine, and spend late afternoon at the beach—not reasons to turn in early. I stifled my laughter, holding my napkin to my mouth pretending to wipe off food.

"Are you in training?" Bruce, the blue-eyed man, asked, hearing that we were athletic. "Tomorrow we're going to bike twenty miles and swim three. We did a ten-mile run today. We're training for a triathlon at the end of the summer."

"That's impressive," I said, thinking about my own puny biking and swimming experience.

"Can I call you next time I come out? We can go for a swim or play tennis," Bruce said. Although I was not ready to date, I gave him my number to avoid explaining why I wouldn't go out with him.

The skin hidden under my clothes was still bright red from third-degree burns. The grafts made my arm and stomach look like a patchwork quilt. I hid this knowledge from strangers and friends and intended to do so for the rest of my life. I could barely stand looking at myself in the foggy beach house mirror. There was no way I would let anyone else see my body.

Bruce called a few days later. "Do you want to go for a bike ride this weekend?"

"Sorry, I have friends coming out," I said. He didn't know mine was a collapsible clunker, and I would be alone and preferred that.

He called again. "Do you want to grab some sandwiches and hang out at the beach?"

"Sorry, I'm busy," I said. I only went to the beach early in the morning or very late in the afternoon and never basked in the midday sun, the heat harmful to my tender skin and recalled being on fire, making me feel suffocated. Whenever he called again, I was returning from a tennis lesson. He asked for a match. I always turned him down.

On a sweltering Friday night, he called once again. My little cottage felt like an oven. Turning the pages of the book I was reading made me sweat.

"Do you want to go out for ice cream?" he asked. I could taste the coldness sliding down my throat.

"Is your car air-conditioned?" I asked, hiding my excitement at the thought of relief from the heat.

"Of course," he said. "Tell me where you live, and I'll pick you up in half an hour."

My skin itched in its confinement. I agreed, removed my Jobst, and wrapped myself in silk clothes. He'd come to my rescue without knowing it.

Sitting in the ice cream parlor, I said, "You may think I'm playing hard to get. I'm sorry. I'm not ready to date. I was burned in a fire a year ago." I expected him to choke on his cone and quickly take me home. Instead, he looked at me and said, "I would never have known. I'm so glad you survived." My chocolate ice cream melted.

Pre-fire, all my boyfriends had been artists, musicians, or adventurers. Now a good-natured, balding man ten years my senior, clad in polyester and white patent leather loafers, who worked for a large corporation in charge of sales, and did triathlons sat before me. We had nothing in common. Bruce was not someone I would ever have gone out with in the past. Yet his kind words made me want to spend the rest of my life with him. His response to me revealing my secret made everything else about him unimportant. He conjured up the safety and being taken care of I felt while recuperating in my parents' house.

We walked on the beach, galaxies overhead. Every now and then, he bumped into me, brushing me with his hand. Then he moved away, as if he had lost his balance. This sweet, shy man liked me. I was smitten.

I wanted to know all about him. "Where did you grow up?" I asked.

"Forest Hills," he said. Sort of the Queens version of Manhattan Beach I thought. "What about school?" I continued. "Baruch," he said, looking down. He didn't ask me any questions or talk much. "What about this triathlon? Why are you doing it? I guess you're into races, huh?" I tried to draw him out.

"I just want to be able to finish it. I'm not into the competition; I'm just proving to myself that I have the endurance," he said. He had a quiet nature. It was refreshing that he was not full of himself, competitive, fiercely ambitious, and sarcastically witty like the boys I grew up with. Even in sports, he was all about doing his personal best, not winning. He asked me to dinner the next night, and I happily agreed. Jimmy and Jacques's abandonment made me more receptive to Bruce who wanted to extend himself toward me, who asked me what I wanted to do.

That night I dreamed I was on a mission in outer space with several astronauts. A shower of bullets resembling little stars hit us, destroying the spaceship and the astronauts, except for me and one man who looked like Yul Brenner. He turned himself into a solid muscular arrow, and I rode on his back. He fought and was victorious against the enemy. We returned to earth and landed in a convention center in Florida. Everyone was fat and middle-aged, wearing green polyester. I told these people that the arrow man had just made the world a safe place for them. They didn't believe me because they had never heard of him. I woke up laughing and exhilarated.

On our second dinner date, Bruce took me to the American Hotel in Sag Harbor. I wore a long, pink, thin cotton skirt with a white long sleeved tee. I remember this exactly because the clarity of the memory of an event precipitating a life change remains a detailed picture in my mind. Over scallops, I felt his hand under the table slowly climb up my thigh beneath my skirt. I ran my foot up his leg. I felt my body more intensely from the inside than on its raw surface. Our first physical sexual contact awakened a passion that gave me a sense of freedom. His fingers climbed higher. I slumped in my chair to allow their ascent. Two fingers slowly crept inside me. Only my shoulders remained above the table. I muffled my orgasm with an enjoying-your-dinner-partner's-conversation smile. I sat straight up, hoping I hadn't been noticed by the two well-known artists smoking cigars at a nearby table or by the family dining a few feet away. They all seemed oblivious, engrossed in their worlds. We didn't order dessert.

I invited Bruce back to my house. The half-hour drive from Sag Harbor to Amagansett seemed eternal, so we stopped in the dark parking lot of a loading dock. I was totally ready when he lifted my skirt, leaving the rest of my clothes intact. At my house, I changed into one of Aunt Sylvia's donated cotton nightgowns—turquoise, long-sleeved, ankle length—and I would not remove it.

Bruce's desire for me made me feel attractive. I needed him like a life preserver to retain that self-image. For lack of company during the week, I spoke to myself so much that I sometimes couldn't decipher what I was saying. One thing I did know was that the post-fire me was not looking for a man whose main offering was artistic narcissism. I was ready for something different, but not sure if Bruce was the form it would take.

After our next date, I was startled to see him install his elaborate toiletry kit in my bathroom. I thought he was renting a place for the summer, but it turned out to be a weekly arrangement. I didn't give it another thought. At the time, my limited world out east and anyone who entered it had an unquestionable glow.

In the business of beauty products, he not only took his own toiletries very seriously but brought me bottles of expensive perfume and lotions to soothe my skin, which I still wouldn't reveal to his gaze. We spent every subsequent weekend evening together that summer, dining out and making torrid love under my nightgown. I wore my gauzy garment like armor. It shielded my skin, vulnerability, and exposure.

During the week, he called every day. It was comforting to have someone care about how I spent my time and ask me what I had for dinner. One result of being burned was that I was cautious about dangerous emotional and physical risk-taking. Bruce represented safety, stability, and caring. Knowing I would see him on the weekend placed a higher value on my time alone for art-making. I started to paint canvases of objects I found around the house. The lamps, vases, and food blender were not mere still lifes. They became the anthropomorphic embodiment of my desire and sexual satisfaction. Everything, including me, buzzed with energy.

When I occasionally saw people I knew who were also summering in the Hamptons, I felt self-conscious about my Jobst encasement peering out from my clothes and pointing to my difference. I looked odd, an outsider to a hip scene. Yet I chose only to remove the Jobst for romance because I didn't want to lose the scar compression time at that crucial stage. I sacrificed the present for the sake of "normalcy" in the future, feeling solace with Bruce from my self-imposed alienation of others. He did not appear to be part of any scene, especially the art scene, minimizing my risk of rejection and increasing my anticipation of being with him.

One night thunder raged, the wind strong and forceful rattled my windows. The soft radiance of the sky became aggressively darker. With the growing anticipation of the rain and storm, I felt like a victim who knows her assailant is there but can't see him yet. There was nowhere to which I could escape. In need of hearing a supportive voice, I dialed the familiar number. My mother answered. After being in her care for months, I had grown dependent on and cherished the strength of her love.

"Darling, I'm so glad you called. Wait a minute. Let me turn down the TV. How are you? Are you OK, sweetheart?" she said.

"A storm's coming and I feel a little lonely. How are you and daddy?"

"We're fine. Nothing earth shattering. You know I'm always here for you. So tell me, have you gone out with that nice Jewish man again?"

"Yeah. It seems we have a dinner date every weekend."

"You must be really getting to know each other. What's he like?"

"It's hard to tell. He's very sweet but quiet. All I know is that he has a job he doesn't talk about, he lives on the Upper East Side, and he's really into food. He makes little satisfied noises when he eats, kind of like a cat purring."

"It could be worse. He comes from the city every weekend and takes you out? Whatever you're doing keep doing it, darling."

"OK, Ma. I love you. Goodnight."

That was the comfort I needed. I hung up smiling. It was the smile of a teenager thinking: *If my mother only knew. She could never imagine.* Then I thought that nothing would shock my mother, and she just wanted me to be happy, and I was with Bruce. He was seeping into my dreams as a superhero and into my thoughts as a rescuer.

Perhaps I was raised to believe that being taken care of was my birthright; as a female I would not be capable of taking on life's burdens alone. I had to be desirable for a man to take care of me, and a good appearance multiplied my chances—the Jewish American Princess ethos of the sixties that I didn't want to buy into but became part of the fabric of my youth. Repeatedly, as a teenager Jimmy said I was the ugliest sister in the world. Despite logic and bucking the dated ideal, it still affected me.

I knew I was desirable to Bruce, but I still saw myself as deformed. I felt lucky to have a man who wanted me. I was determined to hide my feelings of confusion and ugliness around people. As my mother would say, "Just put on a face." But which one? I thought.

Bruce didn't sense any of my internal monologues. He was a simple man, which was a relief because he didn't analyze anything. Every weekend we indulged in delicious dinners and sex, which made me very content when he was around. However, I had enough free time during the week to question my feelings toward him. In the middle of the night when the devil of doubt appeared, I wondered if it was my lifelong insecurity in addition to my scars that made me feel that Bruce was the best I could do, or was it good fortune that we found each other.

My thoughts decidedly weighed on what was genuinely good about him. Bruce possessed the kind of optimism verging on blind trust that things in general would work out. He was generous with his time, making sure I had everything I needed—and even what I didn't know I needed—before he went off to his athletic event. He drove me to Bermuda Bikes to look at Italian ten-speeds to make my rides faster and more comfortable. His encouragement initiated my small jogs down Further Lane, where I took in the beauty of green shrubbery and mansions. I felt my strength and stamina grow. "I'm so proud of you. Next year you'll be preparing for the triathlon," he joked. He was a nurturer with ingenuous enthusiasm translating into what seemed to be a really good guy. Could Bruce be my Prince Charming dressed as a salesman?

Summer was nearing an end, and I was feeling the weight of transitioning back to my life in the city. By the end of August I wondered if this was a summer fling or something sustaining. I thought I might love him, or perhaps what I loved was the possibility of a shared future with a great guy. Since I didn't know how he felt, I didn't want to bring up the subject and make myself vulnerable.

During the last weekends in my beach cottage, I lounged on my patio, busily combing the *New York Times Arts & Leisure* section for the fall season's upcoming events. Bruce slipped into his turquoise spandex biking shorts and top adorned with bold black letters of an Italian bike manufacturer. He clomped around outside in his cleats as he secured his filled water bottle to his bike, preparing for one of his long rides.

I was looking forward to seeing Laurie Anderson at BAM, a new Fassbinder film, and Philip Glass's "The Photographer" when I returned to the city. Bruce had never heard of any of them but observing my enthusiasm, he wanted to share the experience. He offered to get tickets as long as it didn't conflict with his triathlon weekend. I agreed when he asked me to cheer him on for the big race in September.

In this new territory of being on my own, in my new skin, I had no idea what my life would be like. I followed what was in front of me. It felt safe.

On September 8, 1983, I went with Bruce to watch him do the

third Mighty Hamptons Triathlon. The endurance event was relatively new. Watching hoards of slicked-down people with numbers on their shoulders and thighs, like tattoos, enter the bay in Sag Harbor like lemmings at dawn was weird to me. By the end of four hours, after adopting my old cheerleader mode—screaming encouragement like "Yeah, Bruce, you're an animal"—my man crossed the finish line with a self-confidence I had never seen in him. I was proud of him and felt that if he could apply that kind of determination and tenacity to a sport, he could apply it to anything in his life. Maybe he was The One.

~

AFTER A SUMMER OF SWIMMING, I FELT REJUVENATED AND A LITTLE more accepting of my body. I returned to my Tribeca loft where upon entering there was a small patch of dark brown burnished wood on the floor, a reminder of the fire a year and a half before. Although it had become part of my familiar landscape, before the summer I developed an automatic reflex of focusing my gaze on the walls to avoid looking at it. I don't know why I never thought of having the floors sanded, but I just accepted its presence like a new wrinkle and evidence of my lack of invincibility.

Only through the act of painting did I feel any control over my life, continuing the series of marbleized paintings with trompe l'oeil vignettes. As a reaction to people staring at me during the previous year of encasement in the scar compression garments, I became the painter voyeur of inscrutable scenes, inviting the viewers to join me.

As an artist, I had the same challenges as before the fire with the addition of having lost time, connections in the art world, and the confidence of being noticed, in a good way, just by my presence in a room. The path to get back on track was to focus on doing my work. Shaky about interacting with the world, I found safety in my studio. I needed the serenity and solitude of painting for a while. Since the fire, my painting technique had gotten tighter; the realism more defined and images rendered more rigidly. I realized it was my reaction to having so little control in the world. I was still having dreams in which terrible things were happening around me and I couldn't escape. I put that power into my work, which was my universe, to override the chaos of my dreams.

In my studio, brushing images on canvas, my mind started playing with words: Bandage = Bondage, Scarred = Scared. I was beginning to understand that recollections were triggered by words, and they crippled me. My method to reverse this was to focus on the visceral act of making visual images. The knowledge that I could subdue and erase emotional torture summoned my strength on good days.

Yet the isolation was scary at times. I felt fragile as a person, as a woman. The kind of emotional support I needed to bolster me was different than that of the past. Ideally, I needed a man who could unconditionally be there and hoped I had found it in the promising relationship with Bruce.

Looking back, I realize that my obsessive thoughts about Bruce were really a decoy to the horror of the fire. We'd only been lovers for two months, and although never totally nude, he felt my scars beneath my scanty coverings, gently caressing my sensitive skin. His tongue knew no boundaries in the most hidden terrains of my body, and his desire made me feel sexy. But when I was alone and unclothed, I couldn't bear to look at myself. I wondered at what point he would become repulsed and leave me alone.

In the world outside my head, our burgeoning relationship was easy. I just had a hard time adjusting to his lack of two things that were priorities in my life: cultural savvy and professional drive. I had never been with a man who knew nothing about performance art, art after the expressionists, or atonal music; didn't put his career front and center; or wore polyester suits. However, in a way these things worked in his favor. Based on my past experiences, the price to be paid for having a lover who possessed the qualities Bruce lacked was a man who was not faithful. I couldn't bear that kind of blow to my ego, especially at this point in my life. We might be perfect for each other.

I became Bruce's cultural guide and suggested a Fassbinder film playing uptown. He enthusiastically offered to cook me dinner beforehand in his apartment near the theater. When I said there wouldn't be time, but I was eager to see where he lived, he offered to pick me up to go to the film and then see his apartment afterward. I was flattered that he was willing to go out of his way to drive downtown and return uptown again.

Fifteen minutes after the subtitles began, I felt a weight against my left shoulder. I moved and noticed Bruce straighten his head. Throughout the film, I sensed the twitch of his head unsuccessfully trying to stay vertical. He succumbed to long periods of nodding out. I accepted that not everyone loved the innovative German filmmaker as I did and ditched my expectations of sharing an in-depth conversation after the film on the way to his apartment.

As we approached his building between Second and Third

Avenues, the doorman welcomed us into the highly buffed linoleum-floored lobby. My critical side silently surfaced; the formality of the staff and surroundings made me uneasy, never having known anyone who lived in a place that reminded me of a hotel. We took the elevator up to the eleventh floor and entered Bruce's alcove studio. I was used to no frills, high ceilinged lofts and felt cramped under the eight-foot, popcorn-textured ceiling. To the right of the door was a small kitchen with a free standing, well-used, wooden butcher block table that must have literally weighed a ton. Its sturdiness and dense wood scarred with dozens of knife marks indicated that it clearly didn't come with the generic post-war cookie-cutter apartment. Pots and pans hung from hooks on the wall over the greasy stove, reminding me of the times he recounted cooking for sick friends and his fondness for hosting dinners. Comfortable, worn wooden furniture, and faded cushions flattened by use decorated the living room and dining room.

I asked if I could use his bathroom. Opposite the toilet a wall of glass shelves were crowded with bottles of shampoos, conditioners, and styling gels. Why would a bald man have and display all these hair remedies? Who was this guy? The bottles gave me a queasy feeling, and I walked to his bed, removed the portable hand set of the phone, and went back into the bathroom to call my best friend, Nancy. With no trust in my own judgment or instincts, I had to tell her so she could advise me to flee or reassure me that it was no big deal. I needed a reality check, but Nancy didn't answer. I was on my own, uncomfortable in my boyfriend's apartment with the unfamiliarity of the accouterments that marked his day-to-day existence.

No longer the confident, flighty girl I had been a couple of years before who could dismiss a guy because I didn't think he was cool, I reminded myself that Bruce's loving kindness trumped a hip exterior.

"Bruce, I'm getting vertigo from being uptown so long. Can we go back downtown?" I knew I'd feel better once we were in my familiar territory south of Houston Street. I never would have believed it then, but decades later I would yearn to move uptown a few blocks away from Central Park amd museums.

"Sure, I love downtown. We can get a bite at a neat little place in SoHo," he said.

He was so compliant, not at all controlling and genuinely sweet. I could address the hair product thing another time; out of sight, out of mind.

However, a few days later when we met for dinner, he arrived directly after work in his shiny black suit that gave him the appearance of a car salesman dressed for a banquet. The image not only wiped out my desire to have sex with him, but the suit hid his athletic body and almost obliterated the man who was inside, the one I thought I was falling in love with. The naked Bruce was funny, sexy, generous, and affectionate. I wanted the clothes to match.

A descendant of two generations of women who shopped for their husbands' wardrobes, I never wanted to carry on that tradition, preferring a man with a style of his own. Now I understood my grandmother's, aunt's, and mother's actions in wanting their men to present themselves to the world in clothes that reflected who they were. It was a matter of importance to the women, and the men humored them, not knowing or caring about the difference between tweed and herringbone. I didn't want to hurt Bruce's feelings but pondered how he could use some wardrobe changes immediately. I didn't want him to think I was trying to change his appearance. But I was.

"Sweetie, did you ever hear of Century 21?" I asked as we finished our meal. "They have great designer clothes at 80 percent off. It's sort of a downtown secret. Their men's department is the best. Wanna go?" I said.

"Sure. When?"

"How about tonight? They're open late."

When we entered the store, I directed him toward the rows of 100-percent-cotton Ralph Lauren and Perry Ellis shirts. Then I steered him toward cotton cords.

"These prices are incredible. I won't go back to Bloomingdale's again," he said.

He picked out a wool brown tweed sports jacket he could wear with the cords. I bought him an Italian silk tie to complete the outfit. We went back to my loft where he tried on his new clothes.

"You look terrific," I said and meant it, seeing his essence come to the surface. His image was now one of a low-keyed entrepreneur, someone in the business end of the art or design world, or, as my mother and Aunt Sylvia would say, a real mensch. I ran my hand over his sumptuous clothes and slowly removed them, pulling him down on to the couch.

I had met Bruce at the point in his life when he was looking for a change, his version of mid-life crisis. He wasn't the kind of man to go out and buy a red Corvette or Porsche; triathlons, me and my world seemed to be his answer. He was ready for an outward and cultural makeover with me as his guide. A shopping expedition in SoHo for black cowboy boots and funky shirts to wear with jeans followed. He was getting into his new look by buying Armani and Emilio Zegna suits and suede laced shoes for work or a night out on the town. He took his synthetic clothes to Goodwill.

The simultaneous steps taken to improve my outer self were more dramatic, yet not as obvious as a wardrobe change. We were both involved in the challenges of our bodies. His was the physical endurance of completing more marathons and triathlons, mine the physical endurance of attaining full range of motion of my arm by another alteration to my skin. I scheduled an additional surgery to release more scar bands.

Each surgery made me feel like an oyster without a shell. Bruce was the sheltered harbor to which I could retreat. He was my cheerleader, and I accepted his unwavering presence and support during my recovery as a gift. I also caught glimmers of internal changes in myself that I couldn't quite identify, sort of like a room with expandable walls making space for something or someone to move in.

As the months passed, Bruce became like a multi-purpose sponge that expanded to capacity. He tenderly applied lotions he bought for me onto my skin. This coupled with his apparent attraction to me made my corporeal self no longer feel like my adversary.

He voraciously absorbed the performances we went to, sometimes by osmosis when he nodded out to the hypnotic sounds of Steve Reich's drumming and Philip Glass's *Einstein on the Beach*. I poked him during the concerts as his cultural sentinel keeping him alert. He was my Pygmalion and he loved it, later recounting to his friends the incredible performances he had seen. He bought Laurie Anderson, Kitaro, and Roy Hargrove tapes and declared his attraction to Malcolm Morley's paintings. I was happy to have him as my companion for the events and to observe his efforts to fill the gaps in his cultural experience. However, the part of me that still felt ambivalent toward Bruce was the culturally ingrained undervaluation of a certain softness and passivity in a man, which was also the part of him I loved.

At an art opening, Bruce said, "I don't know why your work isn't on these walls. It's so much better than what's here. Your time will come. And, you are the coolest, most attractive woman in the room. Enjoy yourself." With his encouragement I resurrected my style of wearing a noticeable hat or dress as added camouflage to deflect attention from my scars.

In the art world, heavily populated by creatives absorbed in their own visions and careers and whose conversations ran rococo with insincerity, Bruce was my oxygen tank. He provided air, which I needed more than stimulation. In that world, women didn't flirt with him because he wasn't famous or connected. However, once he mentioned that he sold anti-aging products, a crowd gathered around him. He inevitably promised samples to those he thought were my friends.

When I'd catch his eye or hand at an opening, I knew from his look of admiration or reassuring squeeze that he believed in me for being who he perceived I was. This man enjoyed being my behind-the-scenes team of one.

My situation reflected the broader issue of what we need and who we are in our private lives versus the person we are to the rest of the world; in other words, what are we willing to give up for what we deem a greater gain? Bruce expended his supportive energy, thoughts, and time into boosting me up. I provided the stimulation and was the star in our relationship. I needed him to make me shine, embedding the glow to a permanent part of my persona. I felt my conflict vanishing; although, in retrospect I realize that my conflict had given way to a very willing concession.

How could I not love this guy? I didn't care that his bald pate and lack of bravado didn't exude sexiness to other women. I didn't need arm candy. He made me feel sexy and was an inventive and always ready lover. Bruce constantly tried to dismantle my vulnerability and insecurity; I couldn't do it alone. His glorified image of me strengthened my confidence to move forward with my life and my work and get it out in the world again. He hankered to be part of and was essential to my reconstruction.

Bruce was the constant in my life, a buffer of sorts, the person I could always count on. Everyone needs a best friend, and he became mine. In times of vulnerability, he was the support brace that kept me from falling, even though part of me knew that I wouldn't fall if I were alone. The fact was I liked him being there. In a prolonged, gradual process that took at least six months, inch by inch I exposed my nakedness to Bruce. After I showered, he massaged cream onto the raised texture of my scars, the parts that held the strangest lines and shadows, an act as intimate as making love.

On our first Valentine's Day together, Bruce made reservations at Café des Artistes, one of New York's most romantic restaurants. Beforehand, we made love on my bed surrounded by the silk ties I bought him, a big red satin heart filled with chocolate truffles, and a vase holding a dozen red roses. How much more of a traditional Valentine's Day could you ask for? I wore the pale pink, silk lingerie he bought me to replace Aunt Sylvia's turquoise shrouds. He looked at me nervously.

"Brahna, I want to ask you something. I really love you. Will . . . "

"Are you going to propose?" I interrupted.

He was so jittery he didn't notice me blinking back tears. He shook his head in affirmation, looking more apprehensive. His Adam's apple moved as he swallowed and prepared to speak.

"Could you go down on one knee?" I asked, shocking myself. I needed that pose to complete the whole Valentine's Day scene.

On one knee, he took my hand and solemnly said, "Will you marry me and be my wife forever?"

"Yes, yes, yes," I replied. I was no longer in a Hallmark fantasy, but a much better reality.

He released an enormous sigh. "Thank you," he said. "I want you to pick out the engagement ring," he said. "I didn't want to buy you something that wasn't just right, and I didn't know your ring size. Let's go tomorrow and do that. Now we have a dinner celebration to get to."

As we entered Café des Artistes, near Central Park, the bustle and frantic energy of the city disappeared. This bastion of old world charm was filled with a whispering hum, lush floral arrangements, low flattering lighting, and murals of rosy naked youths romping through romantic landscapes. When the waiter approached our corner, Bruce said, "A bottle of good champagne, please. We just got engaged." His voice was a little louder than necessary and filled with pride.

"Very good, sir. Congratulations to you both."

After the waiter disappeared, an older man sitting next to us with a much younger woman whose cleavage poured onto the table leaned over, raised his glass, and said, "Congratulations." Looking at Bruce, he added "Aren't you nervous about losing your freedom?"

"The only thing I was nervous about was that she wouldn't say yes," Bruce replied.

I squeezed his hand. This was the stuff a husband should be made of. Over dinner, we decided to set our wedding as close as possible to mark the one year anniversary of our American Hotel date.

The next morning I called my parents to tell them the good news.

"Darling, I'm thrilled. Of course we'll make the wedding," my mother said. "What do you have in mind? Remember, you are close to thirty-five, and a big showy wedding would be inappropriate. That's for young girls."

"I don't know. I certainly don't want a traditional Jewish wedding in a synagogue but maybe under a chupah in an outdoor setting since we want to get married in July."

"So soon. We should go look at places next weekend. I'll do some research." None of the venues worked out, so my parents suggested I design my own wedding at their house.

As many brides do, a week before Bruce and I got married I panicked. It wasn't the kind of wedding I wanted. I didn't want it to be at my parents' house where I recuperated from the fire. I didn't want to live with my husband in my loft—the place where I was burned—leaving no space to make art.

As I dressed for my wedding in the yellow room of sunny floral wallpaper, across the hall from the gray one where I had recuperated, I had a private conversation with my deceased Grandma Celia.

"Hi, Grandma. I wish you were here so much to see me marry and to dance at my wedding. He's good and kind and yes, Jewish. I love him and you would too."

My reflection in the mirror looked like a doll in an interesting bridal costume. Though I helped my friend Peter design the deco-style, cocktail-length, white silk dress with a high collar and glass beads, I didn't feel chic. Topped by a small white hat and veil with a white, downward-curving ostrich feather covering the scar peeking out on my neck, it wasn't really the glamorous look I sought, just more camouflage.

I didn't see myself. Had the non-conformist been cremated? Wherever she was, she'd have to join me soon if she wanted to be at the wedding, otherwise the unrecognizable reflected image would be the one getting married.

My father escorted me toward the portable chupah, a cloth canopy with four poles held by Jimmy, Jacques, Bruce's brother, Jack, and his best friend, Larry. Bruce was waiting beneath it, facing the Rabbi. My father handed over the mantel of my care to Bruce, who would keep me safe so I could flourish.

We celebrated my birthday in Venice during our honeymoon. This was the third birthday since my accident, and I took the day seriously—a marker for me of the distance I traveled from death to life. At the hour we were seated on the patio of the restaurant Bruce had chosen, the damp air was cold, the darkness made the canal look like an abyss. The staff rushed our dinner, and there was no dessert left, no birthday cake. I was so upset I took my marriage jewelry off my left hand and threw it on the table. "Don't you know how important this birthday is for me?" I scowled at him. Yet at the same time, I observed myself behaving like an entitled child. I didn't understand my own behavior. Bruce looked at me, hung his head, and said, "I tried." Did my existence on this planet, marked by the day of my birth, still feel so precarious that I needed everything to be how I thought it should be to solidify it? Was it because I wanted this second chance at life to be perfect and it wasn't? I wondered if my huge mistake was marrying a man who didn't make each moment magical, and I couldn't accept his love as he was. Or maybe I couldn't accept that it was impossible to write the script for my life and that many moments were not perfect.

I couldn't hold him responsible for every detail of my fantasies. Back in the hotel, I asked him for the rings, which he had put in his pocket. Ashamed of my outburst, I said, "I'm sorry, I'm sorry, I'm sorry. Please forgive me." He did.

9

EXPANSION

A PHONE CALL FROM JANE WIENER, THE FILMMAKER, pulled me out of the isolation of my studio. We had been communicating on and off for months since our first conversation.

The first thing I noticed upon entering Jane's compact West 10th Street apartment were photos of her with other recognizable filmmakers taken in the French countryside, remote mountain villages, and other exotic locations. These framed scenes leaned against books on crowded shelves like welcome guests resting after returning from their travels. A poster of one of her films hung on the wall, staking her claim as a filmmaker. I instantly wanted to be involved in this world, learn a new creative form with which to reinvent the worst day of my life, releasing me from the psychological bondage of the fire. Instinctively, I knew this was an important part of my healing process. Who knew where that knowledge would catapult my life?

"Thanks for coming over," Jane said. "You're looking much better. Actually you're glowing."

"I'm on the mend and just married a wonderful man. Maybe that's why." I said.

"That's amazing news. Tell me about him," she said. I felt a sudden surge of relief. The light went out of the neon sign I had seen flashing in her eyes, reading burn victim, and shifted to amiable curiosity coupled with the eagle eye and ear of the documentarian.

"He's a good man, who's super emotionally supportive. Not an artist; works in sales for a corporation that makes beauty products. I think he's living his creative fantasies through me."

"Sounds cool. I have to meet him sometime," she said offhandedly.

"You will. Did you call me over to work on the grants?"

"I submitted them and none of the projects got funded. I'm scrapping mine because I'm up to my ears with work on industrials—my bread and butter."

"So it's over?" I asked softly and shakily. My spirit and the fantasy of a new artistic venue began plummeting. Yet a moment later, Jane said that if I wanted to make my short film, she would produce it and guide me without a fee. I just needed to raise money to pay for film, a camera man, actress, editor, film lab, special effects, and anything else that came up. I had no idea how to proceed with that but fearlessly felt I could find a way with her at the helm of the project. Before expressing my gratitude, she added that as an instructor at The New School she would get me into a script-writing class free of charge. She emphasized how much I would learn. I didn't need to be convinced. Her thin lips hinted at a smile breaking her no nonsense demeanor. The reason she had asked me to her apartment that day was to be sure of my commitment to making my film. We walked over to The New School where she enrolled me in the class.

She had provided me with a map for my next project. I felt extremely fortunate for the gentle push of momentum and the realization that my self-consciousness as burn victim in her eyes had almost prevented me from going to her apartment. I was the one creating my own obstacles and projecting my fears onto others. I now understood Jane was an ally. She was not going to parade me as a poster girl for the good works of New York's Bravest, as I feared. Still, this knowledge, which I tucked away as reassurance, didn't override a future of recurring hypersensitivity to the effect of my skin's appearance on other people.

The syllabus for the class was great, a new world to learn about. I read everything required and suggested. Ironically, my short film would have no dialogue. The written script would fill in the details of the visual storyboard I had painted a few months back, thumbnail miniature sketches for each scene, describing the action. Thinking of my eye as a camera, I started with an outline—my own prescribed healing process—which, in the short run, would produce self-inflicted pain by reliving the trauma in written description. By objectifying the emotional and physical torment I'd been feeling for almost two years, I would also separate from it. A quote from Mahatma Gandhi sustained my path: "A burning passion coupled with absolute detachment is the key to all success."

I became an observer recording events, a character outside

myself moving through her morning rituals, the only person in my eleven-minute short film. My eye became a camera as I wrote. It focused on the morning light entering my bedroom.

In the outline, the woman wakes in the pure whiteness of her room, a white cat cuddles against her leg. The character stretches slowly. The cat jumps off the bed, jolted from her own slumber. The camera records the transition from peaceful sleep to the woman's face expressing the blind optimism of a new day. She moves as if in a trance, preoccupied with her thoughts. Slipping on a pastel silk kimono, she glides into the bathroom for her morning ablutions. Through a reflection in the mirror, water cascades over her face.

Pan to the large open loft space, focusing on my paintings leaning against the white painted brick walls. The eye of the lens moves across the view outside the loft's windows: a warehouse across the street is blurry in bright faded light as the trucks rumble down the cobblestones. In the next scene, the character enters the main space dressed in painting clothes, different from the pink chenille top and black pants I had worn the day of the fire that had been transformed into ash. She wears a green painter's jumpsuit like the one I had worked in as a scenic painter. Slowly and methodically, she cuts fruit on a wooden chopping board, grinds coffee and places it in a paper filter, and turns on the stove under a glass kettle.

Her arm reaches for the kettle of boiling water to pour into the filter. The flame attaches to her sleeve. I don't remember what happened to the kettle. Did I put it back on the stove? Did I turn off the stove? Did it fall or tip over, maybe shatter? Did I leave it on the counter? I wrote that she put it on the counter before noticing the flames. In the next shot, she runs out into the dark concrete hall with flames spreading over her clothes. Her screams overwhelm and muffle the voice of another person out of view. The sound of sirens joins the cacophonous symphony. There are several frames of all-consuming fire starting in bright reds and oranges and moving down the color spectrum to yellows, which grow more and more pale until the last shot in which they become a blinding white light. Through special effects, I would achieve these images and have the final one appear like the oculus I saw in the hospital.

I drank a large glass of water after writing the outline for the script. Still thirsty, I felt lighter. That night I dreamed there was a fire in my house. In the dream, I was sleeping and heard sirens and felt panic. Somehow, I left unharmed and didn't have to go through the flames or smoke. I woke up sweating.

✍

I BEGAN THINKING ABOUT HOW I WAS GOING TO RAISE MONEY TO make the film. I was living on my savings and painting the marble series in hopes of securing a new gallery. While reading the Style section of the Sunday *New York Times,* I scanned the pictures of people at galas. I tried my own version of a fundraiser at Danceteria, a hip club owned by Jimmy's friend Rudolf. Although musicians I knew played for free, I didn't have the skill of raising money for a benefit. The evening was more of a party, and I walked away with about a hundred dollars.

After trying to be invisible for two years, I was ready to be seen and heard. It became apparent to me that I had the courage to present myself as I was, with a clear mission—people like Jane and Martha Wilson, the Founding Director of Franklin Furnace Archive Inc., who would let me use her institution as my non-profit umbrella organization the next time, and my creative friends would recognize it. They supported me in ways that fit their willingness, capability, and comfort.

✍

TAKING ANOTHER UNEXPECTED TURN FROM MY PRE-FIRE LIFE, I was now open to finding ways to earn money and finance the film. New York City public schools needed teachers. Although I didn't have a masters of education, I had enough other degrees to enable me to teach for a year and then obtain the credentials. A Junior High School on East 12th Street between First Avenue and Avenue A put me in the hub of the graffiti art scene and Keith Haring's home base.

As the new teacher, the principal gave me the classes no one wanted—kids with behavior problems, learning disabilities, and whose primary language was Spanish. My major for the first six months of college was Spanish. I had no problem speaking and being understood when I had traveled to Spain and Mexico. Bring on the kids. How could they not love art?

The classroom turned out to be a hostile, strange environment. When the bell rang, a hoard of screaming teenagers streamed into the classroom, pushing each other, laughing, flirting, putting their feet on the desks or in the aisles to trip each other, and ignoring me.

Some carried boom boxes on their shoulders. Yet it was my room and my domain; I had to set the boundaries. I wrote my name on the blackboard, staking the territory, and filled a closet with all kinds of art supplies and art picture books.

I needed to draw upon a skill set that lay dormant, and I needed to do it fast. After fifty minutes, my class of twenty-five pupils left, and a new group entered. Their average age ranged from fourteen to seventeen. The average age of a New York City junior high school student was twelve to fourteen. These kids were bigger and louder than I was.

"This is art class, a place to express yourself," I said. "There are no mistakes, only solutions." I heard shouts of "yeah" as they absorbed themselves with graffiti, tagged their names on books and walls, and carved them into the wooden desktops—leaving their marks like dogs peeing.

I let out a loud whistle. "There's a time for that but right now I'm going to teach you how to make colors vibrate by choosing the right ones to place near each other." They started vibrating their bodies lewdly. I held up circles of primary and secondary colors but they didn't pay attention. My approach to color theory wasn't working.

I covered the entire back wall of the classroom with white butcher paper and gave permission to anyone who had the urge to tag to do it there whenever they wanted. At first, the entire class pushed and shoved each other to find the biggest space on the paper. When I didn't stop them and there was nowhere left to make their marks, they slowly returned to their seats. They directed their attention toward me at the front of the room, bewildered at what I had permitted. I handed out color wheels, and I shouted out colors and asked them to tell me if it was primary or secondary. That lasted about ten minutes before boys began break dancing at whim. It was infectious. The room filled with whirling dervish homeboys.

"OK," I said. "If you want to break dance you've got to be really good. I'm going to bring my camera tomorrow and take pictures."

The next day, I greeted my students with camera in hand ready to take photos. With the lens pointed at them, less than a handful of boys strutted to the empty aisles between the rows of desks and started breaking. A heavy boy squeezed himself halfway into a coat locker and watched the show. I clicked continuously.

"Anyone want to get on the desk and show me what you can really do?" I asked. "Can you turn on your boom box?" I asked a boy who was about to stand. The room went silent in shock, then music blared.

Two nimble boys jumped on desks, spinning on their heads, legs in the air. No one could compete with them. I captured the inspiring minutes on film. After that day, the students greeted me with "yo" when they entered the classroom, settled into their seats, and focused on the assigned projects. Weekly, I wrote a page simplifying a description of a movement in art history, copied on purple-inked mimeograph paper, and handed them out. Everyone smelled it before looking at the words. Some read about how van Gogh exiled himself, went crazy, cut off his ear, and made paintings like no one had ever seen before. I asked them to make a painting of something they saw every day in the style of van Gogh.

At first, the kids opted for markers instead of paints, but eased into the liquid medium when they discovered what they could do with it. They learned to paint self-portraits, their sneakers, or their friends in the pointillist style of Seurat; the whirling brush strokes of van Gogh; and the optical illusions of Op Art.

I revisited color theory by handing out different colors of tissue paper. They cut out shapes, and as they glued the papers together, the wetness made the paper bleed and new colors formed.

I asked them to bring in magazines to add to my supply so they could make collages of images they liked. For the holidays I showed them how to fold a rectangular paper in eighths and cut into the creases. When they opened them, each was a different pattern, like a snowflake cut-out.

I hung the tag wall in the hall as a class mural and replaced it with fresh paper in the back of the room. There was no great rush the second time. Kids just went to the wall casually when they got bored or antsy, tagged and returned to their seats.

In my studio, I started my own paintings of the break dancing boys with overlapping, sweeping swirls of color indicating the energy they generated. They were figures lost in space trapped in their own orbits. My body loosened and danced while making those six-foot paintings.

I taught the kids that above all else, art was a process of problem solving. You could always change what you did to make it better: make a closer resemblance to what you had in mind or come up with something new that you hadn't thought of. When a girl, painting a portrait, said, "I messed up. I didn't leave room for the mouth," I whipped out a Picasso drawing with the face reassembled in several directions. "You can either start again," I said, "or have fun with the great work you've already done. Try putting the mouth somewhere else, play with it." She made her own version of a cubist face and proudly held it up.

When someone started distracting the class, told "your mama" jokes to put each other down, or taunted me, I said loudly, "Keep it down and pay attention, or I'll step on your sparkling white sneakers." I didn't know if I would have had the courage to do it, but the threat was never challenged. No one wanted a scuff on the sneakers they saved for months to buy. Motivation problems arose every day. One seventeen-year-old boy lived with his girlfriend, who was older than me. They had a baby he had fathered. "I don't see the point in wasting my time making pictures," he said. "I want to be out in the streets making money for my family." The kids bragged about their street lives, and I knew he was a go-between for drug dealers. I also sensed he was a really kind boy.

"What does your baby look at in the room?' I asked. "Me and his mom," he answered. I gave him a green dayglow piece of paper. "Why not draw something he can look at and put it on the wall near the crib. Then he'll know his dad is cool and always with him." Surprisingly , he agreed to do it and drew the baby's name in bubble letters, filling each one in with a different color marker.

One winter day during a snowstorm, someone opened a window and took a handful of icy snow from the outside window sill. Forming a large snowball, he threw it against the center of the blackboard. I was standing to the side and he didn't aim it toward me, but as I watched it melt and drip down the board, the impulsiveness of the action made me realize that no matter how many solutions I came up with, there would always be unpredictable problems. Life was like that, but what if I or someone else had gotten hit? I didn't want to become one of those teachers who saw the classroom as a battle zone and constantly screamed at her students, thinking it would give her authority. I loved the kids but couldn't commit to the random behavior problems for more than that year. I told the principal I would not be returning after June. Little did I know that the year of teaching would be a learning lesson for me decades later.

10

FROZEN MOMENT

I N 1984, RONALD REAGAN WAS RE-ELECTED PRESIDENT OF the United States. Members of the art community mourned the prospect of having the movie star as leader of the free world for another four years. We assembled at Franklin Furnace at an event resembling a wake. I noticed a cool, cocky-looking blond man in a leather jacket surrounded by people. "Who's that?" I asked my friend Martha Wilson, the founder and director of the non-profit organization.

"That's A.M. He's a British composer, super talented, worked with Pink Floyd for a bit and now does avant-garde pieces. Let me introduce you. If you're lucky, he might be able to create the soundtrack for your film. Talk to him."

A week later, he arrived at my loft. Bruce was at a desk at one end of the long room; I showed A.M. my proposal and story board at the other end. To my amazement, he said, "You were burned more than you know. And I don't mean the few small scars. You are a pitiful victim. This is just a feminist film. I don't know why I extended my stay to meet with you."

I was reeling as if pushed back into the flames. Why didn't Bruce get up and say something? I saw my husband's back twitch and ears redden, but he didn't move. Before throwing A.M. out, I summoned my strength and said, "I am not a victim. I am a survivor. I want to recreate that past as the director, the one in control. That way the past will not control me. Get out. I will find someone else to work with."

Bruce got up after he left and held me as I crumbled.

"The man is a beast. You can't take anything he says to heart. He's a moron, an idiot. I didn't interfere because you needed to stick up for yourself and you did fantastic. I love you so much."

Somehow, I did not feel comforted. I just wanted to correct Bruce's grammar. I wanted him to be my shield. I didn't expect him to defend my work, but he certainly could have said something to the man who just told his wife she is a pitiful victim. My husband probably didn't want to acknowledge a comment he truly deemed ridiculous. Yet how could he think A.M.'s words wouldn't devastate me? Why didn't he come to my rescue?

Insecure, I sensed my own imminent collapse and disintegration and doubted my work. My thoughts about making my film, to paraphrase Leo Tolstoy, were that art is a microscope fixing on the secrets of my soul; more pointedly, art is my vulnerability showing people the secrets that are common to all. As close as we were, Bruce couldn't understand what was going on in my head. Maybe my film was pathetic, too literal, and too personal. Should I take the essence of my personal experience and translate it to an art form manifested in a different way? Be less honest? Get more outside of myself to move toward ART? What is ART? For me, making ART about ART was meaningless, a frivolity to keep people's minds busy and off the deeper personal stuff. This wasn't a feminist film; it was a retelling of an experience about life, death, and rebirth experienced by a woman. Maybe he couldn't relate to my voice. Pity wasn't the reaction I wanted at all. How can any reference to someone's personal trauma be a mistake?

I couldn't stop thinking of A.M.'s words all night, lying awake and wondering why they commanded so much of my attention. Perhaps it was because, aside from Jane, he was the first impartial creative person to read the script and see the storyboard. His feedback was unexpectedly brutal. Maybe it was because he was successful and revered in his field, and that status gave his remarks heft. I even considered what he said as unutterable truths, and the shock of that jolted me to consider their credence. Was it because he symbolized to me the conglomerate of all male artists that have made me feel second rate, and I still gave away my power to that opinion? Was it because he had composed sound tracks for many films and if he said he didn't believe in the film and it wouldn't succeed, he was right? And did he really stay over on my account, and if so, I understood his disappointment upon entering our domestic nest and being welcomed by the reality of a husband instead of a purely creative environment and reacting with the purposeful offensive posturing of a rock-and-roll bad boy.

A.M.'s slashing opinion of my work went so deep that I longed for an unrealistic creative understanding from my husband. I felt the worst type of being alone: married to a man I wanted to talk to, brainstorm with, who instead fell asleep while my brain ran wild at 3 a.m.

⟿

TO MY EXTREME SURPRISE, I RECEIVED A PACKAGE FROM A.M. MONTHS after our meeting. There was a brief note of apology for being so harsh and a tape he had put together that he thought might be a start of an idea for a sound track for my film. Where had that remorse come from? I had willfully pushed our encounter to a dark remote space in the back of my mind, aided by my exhaustion from teaching. Did I need to endure torture before the reward of progressing with the film? Was this my reward? I chalked up his extreme, hurtful rudeness to his personality. After all, he was contacting me. I felt validated. If he wanted to create brilliant music, why shouldn't I work with him as long as it was an artist-to-artist collaboration. What he sent wasn't exactly what I had in mind. I wrote back ideas and sent slides of paintings he could choose from in exchange for his work. We developed a sporadic correspondence, giving me hope that I would eventually have an incredible sound track.

The beginning of the following autumn saw an increase in communication with A.M. We decided that the best way to really figure out what he would compose, according to my aural vision, was for me to spend a few days working with him in his sound studio in the house he shared with his wife in London. I arranged to stay with my friends Tom and Jean in their flat, and in late November, took a turbulent plane ride across the Atlantic, alone, for the exciting mission.

The first morning, A.M. picked me up at my friends' flat and treated me to coffee, croissants, and sashimi. His warm and welcoming approach made me feel like a collaborator instead of someone begging for recognition. This time he was like a different person—sweet and polite. We went to his house in the East End—a solid multistoried home that he shared with his wife, much grander and bourgeois than I had imagined. The basement was another world, outfitted with a sound studio that resembled a laboratory poised to discover and release music previously unheard. In this cave of creativity, I learned about the process of making a sound track, adding to my knowledge of interdisciplinary art-making. The black and chrome room was packed with all kinds of equipment, which lacked any familiarity to me, including a huge elaborate keyboard equipped with every instrument built into it. My only aural requirements were a saxophone toward the beginning of the film and the cries of whales toward the end. I had brought a cassette of the songs of humpback whales. The rest was just emotions I wanted A.M. to translate into sound. He made some phone calls, and saxophonist Davey Payne, whose band had a number one record on the pop charts, agreed to do the sax part on the track the next day. Honored that the first thing anyone would hear as the film began was the clear notes of a professional of high standing, elevated the whole piece. I was wildly impressed with the quality and speed in which things were moving along and a little drunk with the power of saying what I was feeling, which A.M. paid attention to and made real through the sound dialogue of the film.

Davey Payne's other-worldly sax was the embodiment of what was in my head as I visualized and remembered my optimism on waking the morning of the day of the fire. Listening to him play in that London basement reminded me of my weakness for musicians. Yet once the music stopped and the other chatter started, the hazy fantasy was gone.

In the studio, we played around with sounds for each cell of the storyboard, which A.M. posted on the wall. Every minor decision was important in sequencing the eleven-minute film.

Listening to the background music, the images and lighting in the film crystallized in my mind. For the very beginning, I visualized a bright light behind the working title *Fireworks*. This bright light, emanating rays so blinding you'd want to reach for sunglasses, would then change to a softer morning light. I wanted the same radiance in the beginning as at the end.

Over dinner with A.M. and his wife, he told me his reaction to my film in New York was because he didn't understand why I wanted to make art replicating a terrible experience head-on. I tried to explain to him that recreating what I had gone through objectified the day. It was necessary for my psychological healing and artistic growth to use a medium that moved through time because it was the only way I could take control of the event that ·changed my life. It hadn't occurred to me then to write a book as a way of healing.

A.M. added music that sounded like Vangelis. He laid down tracks reminiscent of classic Japanese music for the cells where the water was boiling. During the moment of highest pitch, he added the whales' songs. The sax followed; life replacing death. I felt renewed hearing my pain and helplessness translated to sounds outside of me. I relived my experience in the safety of a director's chair in a London basement.

When I arrived at the studio the morning of the last day, I felt at home there and in the East End. A.M. had been working for hours. His unshaven blond stubble and red eyes indicated an all-nighter. I listened, entranced. This man initially made me feel like my idea was worthless and then worked ceaselessly to make the most incredible soundtrack possibly imagined. I felt legitimized in my endeavor to complete this creative project. I loved my first taste of directing and didn't want to leave the immersion in this place of connection with an artist who heard me.

He asked me which of the paintings offered him as payment was my favorite. I told him "Classroom #4," one of the paintings of my students break-dancing.

"I fancy that one," he said.

"Do you really like that the best?" I asked

"Not more than the others, but if you like it the best, then that's the one I want because it will be the hardest for you to part with."

He had me all wrong. Since I considered it my best work to date, I wanted him to have it because of the brilliant job he did. Our goodbyes were brief. Those inscrutable Englishmen. You never knew what they are thinking.

As soon as I returned home, I shipped the five-by-five-foot painting to him.

❧

THAT WINTER, I WAS SCHEDULED FOR A NEW KIND OF SURGERY TO loosen the scarring that pulled on the right side of my neck and limited the turning of my head. It would involve injecting fluid into the scar repeatedly until my neck looked like a flesh balloon. The payoff was the scar could be reduced and released, but there was no guarantee to what extent. Although seduced by the outcome of having a smooth, mobile neck, at the last minute I decided against the operation. I didn't want to look like a monster, even temporarily, especially if the result wouldn't be flawless enough to have suffered the ordeal. After so many surgeries, I still had scars and had reconciled myself to the fact that I always would. It was nearing four years since the fire and I was tired of thinking about my burns.

Instead, Bruce and I decided the cold weather was the perfect time for our obligatory visit to his parents in Florida.

"What am I going to call the film?" I said, thinking out loud in the car on the way to Newark airport. This question had been sitting in my mind like a baby who needed a name. "I don't like *Fireworks*. It's too obvious." The sun had just risen; the sky gradually becoming an almost imperceptible shade of soft pale yellow with brushstrokes of pink and blue.

"Look at that sky, Bruce. It's so-o-o beautiful. A fresh day."

"Frozen Moment," Bruce said

"Yes it is."

"How about *Frozen Moment* as the title?" he said.

"Of course. Perfect. You are brilliant. I love you."

∽

NOW THAT I HAD A SOUNDTRACK FOR MY FILM, IT WAS TIME TO focus on the benefit to raise money. El Teddy's, a few blocks from my loft, was one of my favorite restaurants. When I first moved to Tribeca in 1979, it was a steakhouse called Teddy's, which had been around since the 1920s, a notorious hangout for mobsters and extramarital trysts, and an off-the-beaten-track hide-out for celebrities in the sixties. Intrigued by its reputation my father took me there for lunch during the last months of that incarnation. We sat amidst sleazy-looking men in cheap suits accompanied by women in beehive hairdos and overly made-up faces. It smelled moldy, and I didn't eat meat, so there was no reason to return.

The restaurant was bought and refurbished in the mid-eighties, and made into a tapas bar. The new owners added "El" to the black exterior sign that said "Teddy's," installed an awning of Tiffany glass, and painted and tiled the facade to look Gaudiesque. A Spanish artist sunk a twenty-five-hundred-pound replica of the Statue of Liberty's crown in the roof. El Teddy's was born and became a cool local hangout. The tables outside were always packed with artists and margarita drinkers. The walls inside were embedded with fish tanks. The entrance to the coat room was lined with black-and-white photos of Elizabeth Taylor and Richard Burton and their contemporaries snuggling in booths at the old Teddy's in its heyday. The music was upbeat—the B52s, James Brown, Aretha Franklin, Talking Heads. The upstairs room was perfect for private parties and the owner agreed to let me use it one evening for my benefit dinner. I chose a menu and invited people I knew who would enjoy donating money for my film, seeing their name in the credits, and feeling like a VIP at El Teddy's. Not only artists craved public recognition. Since all the people who came knew me, it was easy to present the storyboard and soundtrack. About forty people sat around tables in the cozy room, munching on fried calamari, assorted tacos, guacamole, and sipping drinks while listening, smiling, and being generally encouraging. It was a great night, and I raised enough money to shoot the film.

I knew I would need much more money for editing, finishing, and special effects but was thrilled to begin. The project to objectify and exorcise my horror was one step closer to becoming a reality. I hugged Jane so hard she squealed involuntarily. Jumping up and down, I said, "Call the cameraman and tell me when you two can start. We're doing this. We're doing this."

She gave me that sly, close-mouthed confident smile I would grow to know well and nodded. "We're on our way, honey" she said.

∽

MY FRIEND TERRY BERLAND, A CASTING DIRECTOR, VOLUNTEERED to find me a pre-fire look alike. I interviewed several actresses to find the one that was my idealized persona. Diane Jones, the one I chose, reminded me of a prettier pre-fire version of myself. She was about 2 inches taller than I was, with the same dark hair and green eyes, and had perfect porcelain skin. I was attempting to relive fate and redirect the pain out of myself.

Jane, the well-seasoned camera man Joe King, the actress Diane Jones, and I assembled in my loft one very early morning in order to capture the beautiful light. Jane and Joe had familiarized themselves with my script and storyboard, which we posted on the wall next to the refrigerator. Every painted cell was in detailed sequence and served as a visual blueprint. Jane and I had copies of the outline I had written.

The vision burnished in my brain, I directed Joe to focus on the morning light entering my bedroom bouncing off the white billowing parachutes hanging on the walls and ceiling enveloping my bed, a room swathed for sensual sex and deep dreams. Opal, my white cat, snuggled against the actress' leg. The soothing sound of her snore-like purring prolonged lingering between waking and dreaming. Unfurling from the fetal position, Diane leisurely stretched both arms above her head, pressing against the wall behind her with the palms of her hands—something I could no longer do. Her upper torso lengthened, as mine used to. Diane stretched and elongated her legs toward the foot of the bed, feet flexed. As she rose, the camera caught glimpses of her pale skin set against lavender sheets. She put on a flowing kimono with patterns of pastel-colored fireworks. The camera closed in on the pattern. She distractedly floated toward the bathroom. As she washed, the color of the water picked up the blues and pinks in the kimono. She reached for a lavender towel, which filled a frame. The color sequencing was key to me in the film—a moving painting in my mind. I relived my pre-fire routine exactly, noticing how I had taken for granted the simple act of stretching and the pleasantness of beginning a new day. Most importantly, I saw myself as a character outside myself moving through her morning rituals.

Woody Allen's glorification of the New York City he loved in his movies inspired me. I wanted to capture the beauty of Tribeca, the transfer of goods from the delivery trucks at the loading bays outside my windows. I wanted to show my New York, the New York that a young artist woke to every morning, the gritty New York on which she wanted to make her imprint.

The camera showed the view outside the loft's windows filtered in morning light. The character dressed in a green painter's jumpsuit, the one I had worn as a scenic painter, the vibrant color transitioned well into the next shot in the kitchen with red lacquered cabinets above the counter where she prepared her breakfast. She absent-mindedly turned on the stove.

Her arm reached for the kettle of boiling water to pour into the coffee filter. She put the kettle down and looked at her sleeve. Her contorted face and mouth opened into a scream. She twitched. In the next shot, my character frantically ran out into the dark concrete hall. "Pretend you're on fire, move as fast as you can to simulate the urgency," I said. I had trouble getting the words out but she understood.

Joe shot close-ups of the flame from the stove and had footage of flames from a fireplace to transpose in the editing room, an illusion to ravage her clothes. I imagined the several frames of all consuming fire. My heart started beating really fast. I checked myself for flames.

But on this day, the only real fire was the one in my memory. No one really burned. The fire didn't leave the stovetop. I was not harmed. I breathed deep with the relief of having reconstructed the event as art. Dressing the actress in different clothes than

I wore that day and the fact that she had flawless skin gave me the distance I needed to detach myself from the protagonist. Through my directing, she became the mirror of my emotions and thoughts. Her movements—a silent, meditative dance with no dialogue—propelled her through the first hour of the day that changed my life.

Watching and molding each scene gave me the freedom to notice things like the vibrating visual effect between the green jumpsuit and the red kitchen cabinets in the scenes near the stove. As complementary colors, they added another optical level to this painful piece that I wanted to look GORGEOUS on film, to counteract the deformity that really happened. I hadn't accounted for variables like Opal the cat maintaining her pose and then leaving the bed at the appointed time. Jane held Opal in place, then shooed her off while Joe held the camera on Opal. Their vast experience caught and remedied the many details that I hadn't even considered. Thanks to their flawless pacing, the shots fell into place.

I had the luxury to tamper with memory and reality, replacing both with a painting in motion because Jane and Joe, the consummate professionals, ran every aspect of the making of the film. Collaborating with them was an honor.

✍

TO EARN AND SAVE ENOUGH MONEY TO PROCEED WITH THE SPECIAL effects, editing, and finishing of *Frozen Moment*, I worked as a substitute teacher—mostly in Chinatown, at my request because the children were well behaved. I also received grants from the New York Foundation for the Arts to work with kids designing and making permanent painting installations in schools. By 1989 I was ready for Jane's guidance in connecting me with the professionals involved in finishing the film. We had shot it on film, and Jane felt the best way to complete it was to transfer it to video and edit it in that form on consoles rather than snipping celluloid strips that would snake around our legs by the time we were done.

I reveled in feeling like a filmmaker as I carried the reels of film to Duart labs for processing and conversion. Posters of films by Martin Scorcese, Jim Jarmusch, and others who were inspiring to me, lined the walls of the reception room. I doubted there would ever be a poster of *Frozen Moment* on the wall, but I was certainly in the right place for the processing of my film. Years later after

Duart closed, I received a phone call from a facility in Hollywood that acquired films from the lab, asking if I would consent to adding *Frozen Moment* to their archive. My film is stored with the best.

∽

I SAT IN A DARK ROOM WITH THE EDITOR FOR DAYS, STARING AT small screens, advising him as he created continuity with the footage, picking the best shots that flowed together.

Jane put me in touch with special effects man Gary Becker to create the fire scenes. I sat in a cramped room with him looking at footage Joe had shot of flames. He showed me the different ways of transposing them onto the actress who played me. Most of what he did looked like an overlay, which was not the effect I wanted.

Watching closely to see the most convincing way to create the illusion of fire catching on her sleeve, I became nauseous. I was going for believable realism, and I knew when he got it right because I stopped breathing. I touched my right forearm and it was not hot. It was intact, a reminder that I was watching it happen to someone else and that she really wasn't getting burned. I exhaled deeply. Reliving the initial experience on a cellular level made me dizzy. I was not detached at that moment from the panic I felt when I was on fire, although the experience had happened seven years before. It was very difficult to convey the essence of the sensation while simultaneously remaining disconnected in the present. I became light-headed but stuck with it. The intensity of the challenge produced an adrenalin rush that forced me to relive it so I could see it through movement and color on the monitor, the universal feeling of pure fear fully experienced, then return to feeling myself sitting on a chair watching it.

Next, Gary needed to make the flames slowly consume her body. I watched as she ran from the stove toward the door into the dark hallway. He tried several techniques to meld the dancing orange and red fire with the dashing figure. Eventually he made the flames gradually envelope her green jumpsuit until the woman was no longer visible. The scene was just fire and whale cries. I was shaking, but again the observer. I wasn't on fire but was watching the action on a small screen, wearing purple silk Bermuda shorts, a cotton top, and short vintage brown-and-white cowboy boots. On the outside, I had moved on. I had the power to say, "Yes, that's the EFFECT I want."

That segment of working was so focused that we took a lunch

break. I couldn't eat. Gary pulled out a brown paper bag and took out matzo, two hard-boiled eggs, carrot and celery sticks—in his observance of Passover.

I didn't coordinate this phase of post-production with the Jewish holiday symbolizing freedom, nor thought about Passover's significance in relation to my film and life at my family's Seder a few nights before. Yet the sight of the matzo and eggs made me feel connected to my ancient ancestors' Biblical release from death and plagues.

The next task was to move the bright red and orange flames down the color spectrum to yellows, then blinding white. As we sat at his small desk, Gary filmed a single flame from a votive candle in front of us and proceeded to manipulate that light. His first efforts retained the appearance of a candle flame. I wanted to see something more expansive and abstract. He broke down the colors in the flame and ran them together on the screen. It reminded me of blending oils with a brush, wanting that painterly coalescing from pale yellow to white heat that created an eternal light. The goal was the white light I saw in the hospital after last rites. After several hours, he succeeded. When I left his studio, the sky was turning dark. I didn't notice. The light on the screen had filled my head and that's all I saw.

11

SPRINGS

W HEN SUMMER HIT THE CITY FULL BLAST, I FELT I was suffocating. My burned skin couldn't breathe and locked in the heat, a radiator about to explode. I needed out.

I never imagined then that the simple ritual of swimming I began in Amagansett would be a lasting antidote to the years of struggle to come. Swimming in the clean salt water and air, rejoicing in the extraordinary light and open space changed how I experienced summer and my body. Biking past corn fields and down shady lanes lined with privet hedges hiding mansions opened possibilities of a world beyond my grasp, while I enjoyed the physical pleasures of being a voyeur passing through it. All these delights were intensified in our coupledom when we rented a place together out east. The tenderness and sensations of our lovemaking fluidly melded into what would otherwise be ordinary acts of living. I felt like a butterfly flitting from one temptation to another as if I only had one day to live.

One summer we rented a house on Hog Creek in East Hampton's Springs, the part of the world where my healing had accelerated, where I felt whole. I resumed my daily swim. It was the fifth year of my aquatic regimen, and I realized that when I was physically active, especially in the water, my thoughts didn't get me in trouble. They just came and went.

My athletic husband encouraged my swimming routine, which became more challenging as I tried to keep up with him. I became obsessed with finding great bodies of water in which to swim. We discovered Louse Point. This spit of beach had two sides. Most people settled on the soft sand of the boat side with a view of a small deep green nature sanctuary and the channel where small crafts and kayaks went in and out to Gardiner's Bay. The other side was open water, a spit of sand on Gerard Drive to the left and Napeague far to the right.

It was on this unpopulated side, with less likelihood of scrutiny of my scars, where we pitched our umbrella, laying on the narrow beach covered with rocks and shells under our beach towel. The water ranged from shallow for a while to shallow for a long while. Wading in, carefully stepping over the rocky bottom until it became sandy, my feet caressed the softness at the point where the water hit my waist. The first plunge toward Napeague was the highpoint of my day.

The current carried me along easily, and four hundred strokes covered a far distance both parallel to the shore and out into the bay. Turning around to swim back felt like swimming in place. The sun-bleached log midway between where I started and where I turned around was still faraway. I stroked and stroked but couldn't seem to pass it. People walking on the shore moved much faster than my swimming speed, caught as I was in the swift tide. I amped up my kicking and stroking and headed toward the shore. When my feet could touch the bottom, I tried to walk out of the bay but wobbled in the undertow. Yet there were no waves; the surface appeared calm. The hidden strength of the water and its force humbled me. Yet I knew it was possible to walk out and then re-enter down the beach and swim back to my spot, merged in the movement of something bigger than myself—a body of water.

Feeling loved and satisfied made hanging out with Bruce so much easier than the challenging art world and the people in it. Only with him did I feel totally safe, and I wanted to be together as much as possible. Sex was an opiate, which made me content, comfortable in the softness that covered my edginess.

Yet I had a driving need to communicate through my art. I loved painting and filled notebooks with ideas I couldn't keep up with. But the career part seemed to elude me. I believed only hard work could give promise to my goals and desires. I couldn't stop trying.

I had no doubt my paintings of figures from the 1930s and 1940s frozen in a scene witnessed through trompe l'oeil portals in my faux marble background symbolized that moment when everything changed. Fire had transformed my life. I reasoned that since I contained the fire, I could be the agent of my further transformation. I already saw alterations in my life. Not athletic before the fire, I now exercised regularly to prevent scar contraction. I felt drawn to people who survived life-threatening illnesses. I cheered their progress to recovery much like Bruce cheered friends across a marathon or triathlon finish line.

As my passion for swimming increased, so did the painting of water's energy, movement, and reflections. Water was my source of renewal. I painted sunsets at Louse Point, oils on twelve-by-twelve-inch boards, and I painted quickly to catch the right light. It was my way of incorporating the change from day to night and was delighted that a gallery in East Hampton sold a few. My body of work looked like a group show by several artists, which was not the way to create a style that would mark my artistic identity. Living on the periphery of the art world, I needed to be on the map as an artist. The dialogue between my paintings and the public was tantamount.

I walked along the ocean just after sunrise. I lay down on a ridge of sand the waves had carved out and built like a platform. From there I watched their performance. Through the soft-packed sand, I felt the pounding of the sea beat inside my back deep within my lungs, kidneys, and spine. I watched the waves, their dramatic form constantly changing. I knew I belonged there like the little piping plovers skittering along the water line having no doubt or thoughts of not having the right to be wherever they were. Yet when I left the beach as the sun grew stronger and other people arrived, I was not sure where I belonged, especially because I had the burden of wanting to hide my body.

Five years since the fire, I wanted to be known for my work. I did not want to be stared at. I wanted to be seen.

The Springs, with the looming legacy of Jackson Pollack, Lee Krasner, and Willem de Kooning, was densely populated by artists, none of whom I knew well but whose work I respected. I felt like a little kid banging on a door saying, "let me in, let me in." Then once the door opened, I retired to the fringes, thinking no one knew I was there at all. Yet the bold part of me wanted to enter with the big kids. I forced myself to call every artist I knew well enough to have their number, though felt awkward being the initiator. I invited an artist couple I'd gotten to know to dinner when Bruce came out on the weekend, hoping to establish a friendship. They asked Bruce how he spent his time out east. He told them about his triathlon training. The flaccid-muscled male painter said, "I can't relate to that at all." We slogged through the remainder of the evening with pleasant small talk but never saw them again except at openings.

I worked on a painting of Bruce in the water called *The Swimmer*, using the same overlay of looping, oil stick, and energy lines I had used in the break dancing kid paintings. The energy of the swimmer was in harmony with the flowing energy of the water; the portrait of Bruce metaphorically a self-portrait.

Human frailty and mortality scared me to the point of feeling my stomach and throat constrict. The fact that Bruce had great physical endurance and a positive attitude made me feel his strength as almost invincible. I wanted him to be with me all the time so I could feel grounded and not about to vanish at any minute. Yet while working on the second swimmer painting of Bruce, I became frightened. In the act of creating the image, I made him vulnerable and possibly perishable in a violent sea, which was not my intention. Undeniably, my hidden fears came out on the canvas. After painting him, I went for my one-third-mile swim in the peaceful bay.

THE SUMMER CHANGED AT AN ART OPENING IN ASHWAGH HALL when we bumped into Dennis Oppenheim, whom I had met at the Odeon before the accident and had run into casually but not very often since then. He had bought a house near our rental and invited us to swim in his pool. The first time we went there, Bruce jumped in, but I wouldn't dream of exposing my scars for the pleasure of a social swim.

During the week, I biked over to Dennis's house. "Why don't you take a dip?" he offered. "Oh I just went swimming in the bay. Maybe later," I answered. I was there for the endless conversations about the creative process of artists from Toscanini to Andy Warhol. He casually slipped in gems about his current projects, like the art furniture he was experimenting with, particularly the writing table shaped like an elongated gun inspired by mystery writers.

It appeared to me that he lived like a modern day Picasso. Dennis had several attractive, smart, artsy young women ministering to all the mundane aspects of life so he could just concentrate on being brilliant. In the height of feminism, it was a little strange but in a way understandable due to the man's charisma. His assistant took care of all his business, someone cooked, another cleaned and maintained the house and made sure the sprinkler system for the shrubs and plants was working, and the pool guy came regularly. It was hard to tell what the boundaries of his relationships with the women were, but I didn't care, basking in his quick-witted diatribes.

He emphasized that Jackson Pollack's house and studio were in walking distance from his house, and Pollack's spirit was soaked in the soil. So is his body, I pointed out and asked where he was buried. A group of us jumped in Dennis's car and drove to Green River Cemetery where a monolithic stone marked Pollack's grave. We stood in reverence for a while. A much smaller rock marked Lee Krasner's resting spot. I laid pebbles on it, one Jewish woman artist in appreciation of another, keeping with our religion's tradition.

Dennis and I became buddies and remained so until he passed in 2011. I saw his sweet vulnerable side. We went to movies on a weeknight or met for a drink in a local bar near the bay and talked about our lives. I stopped thinking of him as the lauded one and simply as Dennis. On weekends he invited Bruce and me to his pool parties where along with young artists and studio assistants, assorted friends and offspring, there was always a demigod, and on rare occasions a goddess, of the art world present along with collectors. Lynda Benglis, the sculptor, arrived in a sari with her Indian man. John Coplans, the photographer, was a frequent guest. I was a humble neophyte in this company, a decorative background figure too intimidated to talk about my work or ask anyone to come see it, not even Dennis. As a stimulated observer, I listened to chitchat about diet, exercise, traffic, who someone ran into at the beach or the general store in between the zingers of their latest accomplishments or brilliant observations.

It appeared that Dennis was very random in his inclusivity of who surrounded him. Only later did I realize that although he was so casual in his expansiveness, he had instinctual pre-requisites for making the gatherings appear inclusive when they were weirdly exclusive. I felt special to be included, even as I imagined myself and Bruce as extras without speaking parts.

In his later years, people assumed I was one of his lovers, but I was one of the few women he knew who hadn't had sex with him. Becoming lovers would have caused me too much emotional turmoil to sustain a friendship with one of the most interesting, talented men I knew. I gained more satisfaction in our flirtations, which extended the heat instead of erupting into an extinguishable fire. This way of interacting with a complex attractive man set a new precedent in how I would relate to men with those qualities while remaining faithful to my husband.

That summer gave me the confidence to put more energy into my relationships with other artists I knew, mostly supportive women.

Returning to the city, I invited more people to visit my studio, leading to inclusion in group shows at alternative museums in New York City and smaller regional museums. My work received good exposure, but I didn't have a gallery. Without commercial marketing, the paintings didn't generate much income. Frustrating, because painters of my generation, mostly men, whose work objectively was not more skillful, more clever, or more appealing than mine, were exhibiting in SoHo.

I read reviews of their work, articles about their lifestyles, parties, and restaurants—like Mr. Chow—where they hung out in Italian suits smoking cigars. Luck was quixotic, and qualitative judgments in modern art were hard to measure. Yet why were most of the rising stars men? When I wasn't feeling disappointed or self-deprecating, I was angry.

12

UNDERCOVER

MY GOOD FRIEND JILL HAD HER FIFTEEN MINUTES OF
fame at the Whitney Museum in the seventies when there
was a feminist curator. Since then her work's visibility
had declined. Daily, we bolstered each other's ideas and strategies
that we hoped would result in the recognition we deserved.

One morning she called to tell me that she and several women
artist friends had formed a feminist activist group in reaction to the
current show at MOMA: *The International Survey of Painting and
Sculpture of 1984*. She groaned while naming the exhibition.

Just the mention of the show made my heart beat faster
with rage. Out of 169 artists chosen, only thirteen were women.
The curator, not even considering women, said that anyone not
included in the show should rethink *his* career. I already felt
invisible in the art world. None of the major curators, critics, or
gallerists knew my work, and I feared I'd be excluded from any
recognition ever.

Jill told me that although all the women in their group had
shown in museums, they've had it with the barriers in the art world.
They wanted to invade a male territory and mount a one night show
in the Palladium. The popular club on 14th Street was a showcase
for the art of hot young male artists like Kenny Scharf and Keith
Haring. The owners agreed to let the women of this newly formed
group have the walls of the club for one night. Each woman picked
her favorite artist to include in the show, filling the cavernous space
with fabulous art by women. My friend said, "You're my choice, do
you want to do it?"

"Of course I want to do it," I said without hesitation.

I was thrilled and flattered to have *Look Through Any Window*, one of my large recent marble paintings, hang in the same noisy dance palace with art by women I had admired for years. The club buzzed with the excitement of women acknowledging each other.

About a month after the event, Jill left for a teaching job at a university out west. I really missed not having my main art support buddy within walking distance. However, a few months later I received a call from someone who said my friend had given her my name. The caller wondered if I would like to join the Guerrilla Girls, the collective that had staged the Palladium show. She told me it was an opportunity to turn my anger into action. The invitation was veiled in intrigue, revealed no names, just an address and a bell number to press.

I was a little intimidated yet fascinated by the impersonal spy-like approach. As I traversed the empty dark streets from my loft in Tribeca to a designated Canal Street address, I felt like a secret agent wearing a smart-fitting trench coat in a black-and-white film noir. I rang the bell marked by a number and undecipherable ink-smudged name on a piece of paper behind a plastic panel. The buzzer enabled me to open the battered graffiti-covered front door and climb up three flights of stairs.

I knocked on the door, and a woman ushered me into a coven of feminists sitting on sofas and chairs in the living area of a loft with slanted paint-splattered floors. I vaguely knew one of them. She smiled with recognition. I had met some of the others in the dark at the Palladium months before.

I took a seat in the loft and removed my coat, wrapping it around the back of my chair. A passionate discussion had already begun. Because of a decision to be anonymous in public, the women didn't reveal their names to me until we mutually agreed I would join the group. "We're going to make people take notice of the inequality in the art world through statistics presenting irrefutable facts," one of the women said. It made sense to me.

"We've already done research targeting the gallery system. People love our poster—

THESE GALLERIES SHOW NO MORE THAN
10% WOMAN ARTISTS OR NONE AT ALL

where we name twenty top galleries in two columns of ten."

"We need to do more to confront every aspect of the art world with the cold facts."

Comments sprayed the room.

"Each poster with the same Helvetica font."

"We should be funny too."

"And sexy, high heels not Birkenstocks. This is the eighties."

"We have to be anonymous so people will focus on what we are saying, not on who's saying it," emphasized a woman I recognized because any working artist would. Her amazing paintings had influenced me in art school. However, the art world's patriarchal hierarchy made it impossible for a woman—regardless of the stage in her career to have the same fame, exposure, and financial reward as men on a similar level.

"Wearing gorilla masks in public seems to be working," said another.

I loved the idea of disguise.

I camouflaged my scars with clothing and accessories. It was the perfect time to don the gorilla mask, exchanging personal identity for anonymity, focusing on gender discrimination rather than myself. Comfortable in my disguise, which reinforced my own invisibility, it put me in a safe and edgy place at the same time.

I listened and hoped to be clever enough to contribute to this collective. I had thought my invisibility meant I lacked something as an artist. It was clear now that it was a systemic problem—and not only about me. They asked if I was willing to put in long hours of research, brainstorming on collaborative posters, and plastering them around town. I felt honored to make the commitment, which included never revealing the others' identities.

One of my first actions as part of the group was in the dead of night, ducking through alleys to avoid confrontation with the police as we plastered posters on buildings and lampposts in Soho. It was so dark I fell into a pothole, wheat paste flying out of the bucket and splattering my clothes and mask.

Having become a member of the "conscience of the art world" only three years after the fire, the mask hid my face, which was the only part of me untouched by the flames. Making me unrecognizable, the disguise added another layer of personal invisibility, which felt right at the time.

Shortly after I joined the group, I was reading Rilke's *Letters on Cezanne*. A short footnote in smaller type about the art of Rosalba Carriera (1675–1757) caught my attention. Discovering her and the revelation of her work took precedence, and the book's text blurred. I reread it several times. I wondered why I hadn't heard of this Venetian Rococo court painter known for her portraits. According to the small print at the bottom of the page, she achieved spectacular success throughout Europe in her time. Yet art history classes and textbooks didn't mention her. I had never seen any of her work exhibited, and no one else I knew had either. How many women artists were forgotten after they died or had lived in total obscurity? What a fate!—to create work all your life and not have it live on and even worse to go unnoticed altogether—a nightmare I shared with so many.

At our next GG meeting, I suggested to the group that we each adopt the name of a dead woman artist to bring recognition to her and her work.

Operating on consensus, members agreed, each one shouting a name she wanted.

"Claude Cahun. She was a gender-defying surrealist in the 1920s."

"Alma Thomas, the African-American expressionist painter."

"Vigee Lebrun, a great portrait painter in revolutionary France."

"Gertrude Stein. OK, she's not obscure. But this American novelist, poet, playwright, art collector, and tastemaker lived an openly gay life until her death in 1946."

"Alice Neel, the emotionally charged portrait painter."

I hoped it was a small step in correcting art history. Feeling gratified to contribute, I chose Rosalba Carriera, Rosie for short.

꙳

ON THE DAY GEORGIA O'KEEFFE DIED, I TRAVELED TO PHILADELPHIA as Rosalba Carriera, accompanied by another group member aka Frida Kahlo, for an interview on NPR's *Fresh Air* with Terry Gross.

Shortly afterward, "Rosie" took her husband to the Guggenheim Museum on Valentine's Day. This was the only time I performed a Guerrilla Girl action in plain sight and incorporated a man as my beard to hide my intent. We infiltrated the crowd wearing museum-goer outfits to blend in—he in a sports jacket and cords; me in a colorful long-sleeved dress. We started looking at the show from the top level. Taking turns, we placed a bunch of five-by-seven-inch stickers, showing the group's latest statistics on gendered financial inequality both in the contemporary world and beyond, in the bathrooms. The adhesive mini-posters were black-and-white reproductions of a dollar bill with the following words underneath the image:

WOMEN IN AMERICA EARN
ONLY 2/3 OF WHAT MEN DO.

WOMEN ARTISTS EARN ONLY 1/3
OF WHAT MEN ARTISTS DO.

◆

I BEGAN GOING ON GG SPEAKING ENGAGEMENTS. THE ANONYMITY GAVE
me the courage to strut on stage and speak about inequality
that the world of "high" culture didn't acknowledge. In doing
so, I was very visible, yet no one knew who I was. The gorilla
mask helped me to focus on what I had to say to the hundreds of
people in the audiences at universities, museums, and art centers
that hired us to speak, be it Nebraska, Indiana, San Francisco,
Buenos Aires, Oslo, Dublin. I stood on the stage with one or two
other members of our group, a microphone shoved inside my
latex mouth, enjoying the sexual innuendo and how displaced it
appeared, to the audiences' delight. I referred to the information
on our posters that flashed on a screen. Each one addressed a
problem in the art world.

One, printed on pink paper, targeted art collectors:

DEAREST ART COLLECTOR,

IT HAS COME TO OUR ATTENTION THAT YOUR
COLLECTION, LIKE MOST, DOES NOT CONTAIN
ENOUGH ART BY WOMEN. WE KNOW THAT
YOU FEEL TERRIBLE ABOUT THIS AND WILL
RECTIFY THE SITUATION IMMEDIATELY.

ALL OUR LOVE,
GUERRILLA GIRLS

We trained our statistics on art magazines with the poster:

WHICH ART MAGAZINE WAS WORST
FOR WOMEN LAST YEAR?

It listed the top five, citing that from September 1985 through the
summer of 1986, the percentage of projects and one-person show
reviews of women artists ranged from 13 to 25 percent.

People gasped at the poster of the abysmal statistics on museums for 1985:

HOW MANY WOMEN HAD ONE-PERSON EXHIBITIONS AT NYC MUSEUMS LAST YEAR?

GUGGENHEIM 0
METROPOLITAN 0
MODERN 1
WHITNEY 0

As our anecdotal presentation progressed, I saw questioning and wary faces change to smiles. Roars of laughter accompanied nods of commiseration over the posters of the BAD REPORT CARD on gallery representation and THE ADVANTAGES OF BEING A WOMAN ARTIST, a tongue in cheek list including WORKING WITHOUT THE PRESSURE OF SUCCESS and KNOWING YOUR CAREER MIGHT PICK UP AFTER YOU'RE EIGHTY. People sat up straighter when we offered them suggestions about taking to the streets with facts from their own community. The room buzzed when we advised them to form their versions of our group locally. When a woman said she felt no one would ever see her art, I told her to keep making it and not be discouraged. Her vision was as important as anyone else's. My advice to her was the same as I gave to myself. At the end of the presentation, monkeying around, we tossed handfuls of bananas into the audience. People scrambled to catch our signature symbol. They lined up for us to autograph our posters. They told us they loved us. Then we slipped into the night. When I took off the mask, I felt stronger in myself.

~

A GUIDING HAND HELPED ME AND TWO OTHER WOMEN OUT OF A limousine. Our heads were encased in big black hairy gorilla masks impairing peripheral vision. My short tight dress hiked up my thighs as I extended a leg covered in black opaque tights and a high-heeled foot onto the curb. *New York Magazine* invited us to a banquet for The Power That Will Be award. The honor of being there surpassed the difficulty of eating and drinking since we never removed our disguises.

After the event, I arrived home, kicked off my shoes, slid out of my tights, and peeled my dress off over my head, catching a glimpse of myself in the mirror. I hated that polished surface for it revealed my scarred body, which I forgot about during the evening. Hiding one aspect of me to bring attention to something else was familiar and still a lesson I had to keep learning.

No one in the group knew about the ordeal of the fire I had lived through, and I saw no reason to tell them. Why explain that I could only wear natural fibers like cotton or silk with my newly grafted and sensitive skin? Why explain that I carefully chose my clothes so they would camouflage my defects and look hip yet in the realm of normal? My involvement in the group gave me compatriots and made me feel less vulnerable in the world. After a gig, I sat in a steam room with GG Alice Neel, counting on that heavy mist to act like the anonymity of the mask. The haze of the steam hid my scars from her. With our bodies obscured, we were just the sound of our voices giggling and rehashing the night. Simultaneously, we were both hiding our identity from everyone in the small town who knew that we were staying at the hotel.

Always, the fierceness of the mask remained inside me when I needed to summon it without the disguise. The scars didn't diminish but their importance seemed to.

Years later, Gertrude Stein and I had a gig offering workshops at an art center in San Sebastien, Spain. After spending the day in our masks, helping local artists make posters that were relevant to them, we could swim in the sea in the late afternoon when the sun wouldn't be harmful to my tender skin.

I had been wearing a long-sleeved leotard for fourteen years since beginning daily swims as an antidote to the ravages of the fire. Before the trip to Spain—during which no one I knew except Gertrude would see me—it was time to buy a real bathing suit. We had been involved in "monkey business" (GGs) and been friends since I arrived in New York City. I felt comfortable with her. I bought a one-piece black number with white piping around the cleavage-exposing top and gingerly took off my cover-up.

Once again, I confronted my own inflated self-consciousness. No one paid any attention to my bared scars. All eyes turned to the white-gloved demonstrators on the promenade around the sea. ETA, an armed leftist Basque nationalist and separatist organization, had recently killed a young father. The citizens of San Sebastien formed a large protest against the unnecessary brutality.

When they passed and I registered the impact of the political events of the region, I entered the vast ocean as a cleansing—unnoticed. For the first time, I felt the breeze on my arms and got goosebumps as I dangled them in the water. The feeling of lightness and freedom from swimming unencumbered propelled me faster to the floating raft.

∽

BEING PART OF A GROUP WITH A MISSION GAVE ME PERMISSION TO be a troublemaker, a bad girl of sorts, the opposite of the child who quietly sat on the television stage throne while her brother won prizes for her. Working for the greater good, I could address issues that affected other women and artists of color without drawing attention to myself. Not being motivated by self-gain as a GG, I felt empowered to do more, like any other masked character who leaves after doing the deed. For fourteen years, I anonymously helped stir up the cultural stew of the art world, bringing the ingredients that allowed the most interesting flavors to rise to the surface.

I stood on a crowded subway station thumbing through an issue of *Ms.* at the newsstand kiosk. I opened to an article with double-page photos of women I knew were multi-racial in workout clothes, paint-splattered jeans, and business suits, looking fierce and combative in gorilla masks. There I was, disguised in my little long-sleeved, tight black dress. People were looking over my shoulder. "Are you buying that?" asked the man in the kiosk. "Absolutely," I said.

∽

FOCUSING ON THIS FORM OF ACTIVISM SOMETIMES ECLIPSED TIME for my own art and personal career. Yet I persisted painting. Although my work was separate and not overtly feminist, being in the group added to my commitment to create what was important to me. I gained confidence I could not have achieved in isolation, especially after the trauma of having life as I knew it burned away.

∽

PERHAPS THE GUERRILLA GIRLS' GREATEST INFLUENCE WAS informing, supporting, and encouraging women and artists of color. We created an awareness of the three prongs that control who moves up the ladder: the dealer, the collector, and the museum. Our collective exposed the limitations of accessibility to success and restrictions set up by discriminatory practices.

Over the last thirty years, the art world has changed. In 2017,

MOMA, the institution whose bias ignited the formation of our group, mounted a show called *Making Space: Women Artists and Postwar Abstraction 1945–1968*. When the museum reopened in 2019 after an expansion of space, they included many more works of women and overlooked artists. We had finally outlived Linda Nochlin's 1971 pioneering feminist essay, "Why Have There Been No Great Women Artists?" Everyone now admits that there are great women artists, adding to the thickness of art history books. The percentages are still low, and I find myself still counting numbers of those represented when visiting galleries and museums. However, our presence is more visible, and a visit to MOMA in 2021 proved a wonderful surprise. In the galleries holding the museum's collection from 1970 to the present was art made by women and artists of every nationality. I knew people who were exhibited and didn't need to see my own art on the walls to feel very much a part of the change.

13

GAINS AND LOSSES

B RUCE'S WOODEN BUTCHER BLOCK HAD BECOME A fixture in our kitchen. *My* loft became *our* loft transformed into a warm home. No longer finding pleasure cooking on a stove—its heat and flames making my head spin and my breathing go fast and shallow—I wasn't burdened by any parts of domesticity that made me panic because Bruce loved performing those rituals. Although he worked at a job, cooking was his form of creative expression. On a beautiful warm night after working for hours in my studio on my second painting of the kids break-dancing in the classroom, I felt the beginning of a new phase in my marriage, of a calm understanding of our routine as a couple. He wanted me to gain recognition for my work. I felt fortunate to be able to go home to a dinner cooked by and shared with my husband.

I loved that he cared enough about my safety to pick me up from my friend's house if the hour grew late. I loved being part of a couple accustomed to kissing, holding, and stroking each other, making love, always having a Saturday night date, sharing the everyday simple pleasures, planning for the future together.

Self -doubt sometimes crept into my precious studio hours. Was my work enough on the edge? Yet, since my accident, it was essential for me to feel safe and protected. Bruce provided that. I was free to do anything I wanted in my studio. I needed the process of working to help me figure out who I had become. We rented a large studio in a warehouse overlooking the water in DUMBO (an acronym for Down Under the Manhattan Bridge Overpass, a neighborhood in Brooklyn) and put up a wall separating the space. He had his office on one side and my studio was on the other.

ON A SUMMER NIGHT IN 1990 WHEN I WAS AT CUMMINGTON Community of the Arts in Massachusetts, Bruce called me from the city. On the other end of the line of the communal pay phone, he said "the building in DUMBO had a major fire today."

I let out a gasp. Every time a fire engine was in sight with its sirens screeching I panicked, shook, and checked myself for flames, the trauma still in my bones, easily triggered. I started trembling and breathing rapidly through my mouth.

"Don't worry, calm down, please," he said. "Everyone in the building is safe, including me. The firemen came and not only saved us but your paintings as well. I'm so glad you weren't here." I agreed, shaking on my end of the public phone. He did not elaborate and tell me that many of my paintings were damaged because he knew I would not be OK, and he wanted me to work well for the month since I no longer had a studio.

I would learn when I returned that while sitting at his desk doing paperwork, he smelled something burning. He looked out the window and saw flames and clouds of smoke, felt heat coming up from the floor boards, and saw tendrils of smoke rising. Bruce ran into the hallway and screamed fire, knocking on the doors of people in their studios. Everyone ran out of the building unharmed. Fire engines arrived and the fire fighters extinguished the flames that decimated our spaces and destroyed many of my paintings. Somehow, the studio down the hall remained intact. A few hours later, when it was safe to enter the building again, Bruce and our artist neighbor brought my paintings to her studio and cleaned those that were salvageable and stored them there. A later investigation found the fire to be arson. No one was compensated, and I never went into the charred building. When I returned, Bruce brought my paintings to our loft. They smelled of smoke. I couldn't live with them, and we brought them to my parents' house to store in their basement; once again their home my refuge from a fire.

That incident was the clincher to what we had been considering for a little while. We both thought it would be ideal to have our own house and my studio in an artist-concentrated area, enabling us to spend time-off together with an independent place for me to work. I wanted Bruce close by. Since the Hamptons were financially out of reach, we followed the formula of others, drawing a circle on a map of New York State with a radius of under two hours from the city. Our priorities were swimmable water, low price, and enough land permitting us to walk out the door naked where no one would see us. We chose financially depressed but spectacularly verdant Sullivan County, abounding in lakes and abandoned bungalow colonies from the fifties. In the summer, some of those bungalows, patched and refurbished, were an oasis for Hassidic Jews from Williamsburg, Brooklyn. We knew of many artists who had houses in the area, and it was the former site of the 1969 Woodstock Festival in Bethel, New York. That event was a benchmark for my generation. Everyone had a story about what they did there or why they weren't present.

We drove along Route 17B on the way to see a house on Gabriel Road advertised in the *New York Times*. Passing the sign for Yasgur's Farm, which marked the site of the festival thirty years before, I turned to Bruce. "You didn't go to Woodstock did you?" I asked.

"I absolutely did," he said. "I was in the National Guard at the time to avoid being drafted for the Vietnam War. That was one of my weekends of duty, and I was assigned helicopter patrol, circling Woodstock."

"Are you kidding? You were in an army uniform policing the festival that celebrated love not war?"

"I didn't see it that way. Sure I had the uniform on, but we were smoking joints listening to the music from above. No one in the National Guard wanted to be in the Army or fight in Vietnam. What about you?"

"I was living in California and just happened to be visiting my parents in Brooklyn at the time. My friends Nancy and Jeff, who lived in the city, didn't have room in their car to take me. Going to outdoor rock concerts in Golden Gate Park and be-ins was my thing. Crushed at not being able to participate in this east coast event, my parents, anxious to spend time with me, suggested the three of us make the excursion. I wanted to go so badly, can you believe I agreed?"

"Now you've got to be kidding." Bruce smacked his forehead with the flat of his hand.

"I'm not. Clad in my see-through blouse and bell bottoms, I took the back seat in their Lincoln. They were in their forties then and to my surprise wore jeans for the occasion. 'What are you wearing?' my father asked with a red face when he saw my breasts through my gossamer top."

"I can see Herb being a little perturbed," Bruce laughed.

"'This is my concert outfit. Everyone wears these kinds of clothes,' I told him. 'Leave her alone,' my mother whispered to him.

"As we approached Route 17, the traffic was at a standstill. People left their cars and weaved on foot through the vehicles on the road, talking to each other. It was a giant party on the highway.

"'This is unbelievable,' my dad said. 'No one is honking their horns or getting angry or impatient. What's going on?'

"My generation, I said. 'Everyone is in a mellow mood. Why ruin it?' I didn't add that everyone except me was stoned out of their minds. Then it started to rain.

"The downpour grew heavier, and there was no way that by the time we got to the site we were going to hang out in the rain and listen to music. My parents opted for a nearby motel, and we left the next morning for the city. I never got to the festival, but I was close, and I've always been embarrassed that I went to Woodstock with my parents. I think you are the only person I ever told. Now, somehow it seems so bizarre that I'm not embarrassed anymore."

I couldn't possibly imagine then that as the girl who went to Woodstock with her parents, I would have the much greater embarrassment and burden several years later of burn scars.

Bruce and I continued driving through back country roads lined with mature trees and occasional farmhouses, spotting a cluster of men in long black coats and big black hats and a group of women in long skirts trailing behind. We finally saw the log cabin set back from the road surrounded by five acres of open fields. The owners showed us around telling us that although the house was constructed from a kit, they had added the pink Mexican tile floors, wood burning pot-belly stove, and updated the bathroom with a large Jacuzzi tub. The spacious bedroom upstairs under the dramatically pitched roof had a balcony just big enough for two people to stand on. It faced the pond, which was twice the size of an Olympic swimming pool. The house felt cozy yet larger than our loft. The walls and ceilings were knotty pine on the inside and burned sienna-colored logs outside. We took the owners up on the swim they offered to experience the depth and cleanliness of the pond. Floating in the water, we knew the cabin and property were rural perfection that we could customize. We wanted something new in our life, something tangible to build on, and put in an offer that night.

A few months later, we moved in. Bruce carried me over the

threshold. My father followed in his station wagon to help. Equipped with a silver salt shaker, an old Jewish custom, he sprinkled our entrance for good luck.

∽

To our delight, we learned that Sullivan County was the land of exceptional lakes. Every water had its own motion and distinctive characteristics. The initial finding of those was like finding a new friend and silently acknowledging the mechanics of the relationship. We discovered beautiful, clean, remote Crystal Lake—the destination a secret liaison. Hardly anyone was ever there because the wooded shoreline and interior didn't allow for open spaces to picnic and hangout for the day. I liked the shade on hot summer days and the absence of people. The lake had different widths. At its narrowest, it was a leisurely four hundred strokes back and forth. That was my easy swim. At its coldest and widest, over 600 vigorous strokes. The depth of the water was limitless. Although there wasn't an undertow, the challenge was not thinking about drowning. I surrendered to enjoying being like a buoy in the middle of intense, cool, green deepness.

∽

I couldn't wait to have Jimmy and Jacques spend time with us in our new country house. The disturbing visit in Amagansett seven years before had caused an unexpected shift in our relationship. They had formed an almost imperceptible wall that kept me on the other side. I wanted my brother and our lifelong comradery back. I didn't need him to take care of me. My desire was to establish a sliding door, a portal to reach him and Jacques.

While I was fighting for equality in the arts, my brother was marching on Washington in support of Act Up—AIDS Coalition to Unleash Power. The direct action advocacy group worked to impact the lives of people living with the pandemic of AIDS by bringing about legislation, medical research, and treatment with the goal of ending the disease. As a gay lawyer and humanist, this was a compelling outlet for Jimmy's expertise and political passion in the mid eighties to early nineties. He didn't stop there.

Jimmy became a founding member of the Lesbian and Gay Law Association of Greater New York. He specialized in probate law. He defended the property rights of survivors in gay relationships, resulting in Eve Preminger, a surrogate court judge, legislating law to that effect during a time when gay couples had negligible rights as partners.

Our family holiday dinners were a perfect stage to present our stories of victories and challenges, with my full knowledge that his playing field was so much more urgent and larger than mine.

In April 1992 we assembled at my parents' house for our annual Seder. I was surrounded by my support team of close and extended family, a constant in my life over the last ten years since the fire. I loved these gatherings. Whoever could voice their opinions the loudest received my father's attention and power to engage with him on politics. My belly ablaze with conviction I looked forward to our conversations around the table. However, that particular Seder was more subdued. I had laryngitis. Jimmy had a very bad head cold accompanied by stuffed nose and puffy eyes aggravated by his lifelong asthma. After dinner my mother shooed all of us out, telling Jimmy and me to take care of ourselves, wishing Bruce, Jacques, my Aunt Sylvia, cousins, and Neal, Jimmy's law partner, a happy Pesach. Refusing anyone's offer to help, she said she would clean up at her leisure.

The next morning I was in the shower when Bruce answered the phone. He shouted for me to come talk to my father. Between sobs, Dad cried, "Jimmy's dead...asthma attack...died before ambulance came...Jacques's arms. We're on our way there. Stay put. Call later."

The Hansel to my Gretel was gone. Our loft felt like an island detached from the mainland of my family. I felt abandoned even in Bruce's embrace as I howled "NO" again and again and again.

In his last years, Jimmy circled an orbit that people were frequently dropping out of seized by the plague of AIDS. Many were my friends too; some of my first New York City buddies introduced to me by Jimmy and Jacques. They were the only men I invited to our wedding. Even while mourning the losses, there was always a fabulousness about Jimmy and his world. But he wouldn't let me enter it in the last year of his life. When he was a toddler, I wouldn't allow him into my room to play with me and my friends. When I slammed the door in his face back then, did that rejection hurt as much as the one I felt from him during the last few years? It couldn't have possibly been as painful as the exclusion from his fortieth birthday dinner. Now that he had left his body, I sensed he was in flight but couldn't see where he was or where he was headed.

Unlike many of our friends and our grandparents, there had

been no sign of Jimmy's life fading away. He was forty. His eyesight didn't fail him, or his coordination or hearing. He never lost his ability to convince an opponent to his way of seeing things or to tell a good story. His clothes were not too big for him. He didn't shake or lose his balance. His memory was sharp. He had plans to travel to Paris with Jacques the next month and bring my mother, treating her to her first trip to France. Jimmy had never spent even one night in the hospital. We knew he would have been a terrible patient and would have hated being there.

His sudden demise made his absence too shocking for me to absorb. Only the Jewish rituals of death and burial would cement the reality.

The next day I expected the selection of a casket to be morbid, but it wasn't. We were making plans for Jimmy, taking care of him as a family. My mother asked us if we should get a shomar. "A what?" Jacques, Bruce, and I asked in unison. She explained that in the Jewish religion, you could hire a man, usually an old man, to keep watch over the body from the time of death until the burial. The idea is that a body should not be left alone like a piece of luggage in a locker. Before any of us could say anything, she added that Jimmy would hate it. We all agreed that it would be creepy to have a strange old man sitting next to his body and certainly not Jimmy's style.

His absence was our glue; the tasks and rituals kept my parents, Jacques, Bruce, and I together as a unit, preventing us from falling apart. The following day at the funeral I needed to see him in his coffin before the hundreds of people filled Riverside Chapel. I hadn't seen him dead and wanted proof. They opened the lid for me as I stood alone with him on the little stage of a very large room, which friends, associates, and our family were waiting to enter. I stroked his cold, waxy smooth cheek with the familiar beauty marks. I put an envelope with a note in my father's large scrawl inside the breast pocket of Jimmy's jacket as my father requested, which felt more intimate and invasive than touching his face. I whispered goodbye. Sharing the last moments with his body, which was more like a Duane Hanson sculpture, couldn't make up for the time I missed with him. I was relieved to know he didn't suffer. I knew he was at peace, but everyone who loved him, including me, bore the huge weight of sadness.

The loss of my only sibling left a gaping hole in the verification of my past. We were no longer "the kids." I suddenly became an only child who couldn't reminisce with him about turning him on to his first joint and staring at the microscopic design on the shell of an ordinary egg. He was no longer a phone call away to confirm any odd memory that popped into my head or to tell him I loved him. Sitting at the white Formica breakfast room table growing up, my mother told us that no matter who we fell in love with or married, no one could replace a brother or sister. She was right.

A few days after the burial I went upstate. There was no Shiva period because it was Passover. My parents, overwhelmed by their grief, couldn't bear to see or deal with mine. Devastated Jacques was bolstered by his and Jimmy's friends.

I thought nature would be healing. The freshness of my brother's absence filled the air, although he had never been to our country house. He died two weeks before our planned visit. Even though I missed time with him during his last years, now I didn't know which was stronger—the loss of my brother or my own loneliness; maybe they went together.

I spent hours, days, months, a year in my studio working on four six-by-six foot paintings of the reflections in our pond in each season. Incorporated in the nature imagery were obscured photo transfer images of Jimmy at different stages in his life, for every season without him. While painting, I engaged in all the conversations I wanted to have with him but never did.

Painting the spring with budding trees of pink and white blossoms reflected on the pond's surface, the repeated handsome image of him in his thirties, sweater flung around his neck, sitting in an undefined space, hand on knee holding his signature camel cigarette, about to give good counsel or an engaging story. Working on that canvas, I screamed at him for not letting me into his life at its apex. Did he not think I was worthy of his time? I asked over and over why he didn't invite me to his fortieth and last birthday dinner.

With the lushness of verdant greens reflected in the pond in summer, I interwove repeated pictures of him looking like James Dean, using a photo Jacques had taken not long ago and printed as a thank-you card to all who offered condolences and as a memorial picture of Jimmy. That image produced mixed feelings for me depending on the day. I admired my brother's confident, cool beauty. I screamed at him for abandoning me my first summer in Amagansett. But more than anything, painting the canvas with that recent photo cemented Jimmy's death.

During fall, the pond reflected the brilliant fiery sun and the red, orange, and yellow leaves. Interwoven with the colors was the repeated photo booth image of him and me circa 1978 when we partied together and were both starting our careers. I conspiratorially laughed and reminisced about our adventures traveling together in Spain, Morocco, and Mexico; going to fern bars in San Francisco, telling each other who we thought was cute and seeing if our gay radar was on course; dancing with him, Jacques, and a gaggle of other beautiful young men at Studio 54, Danceteria, Mudd Club, Area. I recalled our secret and blatant hopes for our futures. Then I cried because all that was over.

When the pond reflected the snowy blues and grays of winter, I inserted pictures of six-year-old Jimmy with his skinny neck and slanty smile snug in his pajamas—my childhood conspirator and sometimes rival and nuisance—shedding more bittersweet tears and yet feeling our secure and protective childhood, the pride in being the big sister. We made up games where he was the boss dictating notes to me, the secretary; or Luncheonette in our kitchen where he was the customer and I the waitress. It reflected the roles of men and women at that time and the TV shows we watched like *Private Secretary*. How long ago that seemed. How the culture as I knew it had changed.

Could it be that I only knew Jimmy in relationship to myself, through his interactions with me? Is that how we know most people? I emerged from the studio after each evolving grief ritual exhausted from crying, painting, talking, sometimes laughing at our shared secrets and elated, filled with his presence. After a year, I let him go, feeling pure love without nagging thoughts.

14

CHILDREN

IN THE LATE EIGHTIES AND EARLY NINETIES, I RECEIVED enough money from grants and artist-in-residence programs to paint full-time. The arts in education grants combined my painting, teaching, and art therapy skills. I designed and instructed students in the creation of permanent painting installations in public schools. Most of these students were branded special education kids, which translated to having behavior problems and/or learning disabilities. They were also the kids who were most creatively uninhibited, many with natural drawing aptitude. "Art is problem solving, finding solutions," I told them. "There are no mistakes, just adjustments." I set them up for success not failure.

The kids entered the classroom excited to see what we were going to do that day. I was only there for a few hours twice a week as a visiting artist. The room we worked in was a sanctuary, a separate space away from the over-burdened teachers yelling at them for their short attention span or repetition of doing or saying the same thing again and again. It was the room where they could express themselves through art.

Gangly, sixth-grader Phillip came in and hugged me. "I want to paint Jackie Robinson today," he said. I knew that as soon as he had a paintbrush in his hand and the colors in front of him, he would be hyper-focused on what he was creating, and it would far exceed what was expected from an eleven year old.

As projects developed, I saw physical changes in the students. They strutted or ran into the art room with more confidence, anxious to work on something that showed tangible improvement, something they made happen with their own hands. I felt good about providing these kids with a space where they could feel accomplishment.

Depending on the location and population of the school, I consulted with my preteen crew and came up with a theme that aroused their enthusiasm. For the Raoul Wallenberg School, named after the great humanitarian, diplomat, and businessman, we executed a three-part mural for the lobby. As inspiration, we looked to Wallenberg's courageous actions during World War II, when he issued protective passports and shelter in buildings designated as Swedish territory, saving thousands of Hungarian Jewish lives. We researched other heroes. The students didn't realize that they were learning about history because they were so involved in the whole process. Combing through books, they shouted out who they wanted to portray: Eleanor Roosevelt, Mother Theresa, JFK, Jackie Robinson—Phillip's choice—Louis Pasteur, and Martin Luther King, among others in their murals, which I designed by projecting pictures of the historic heroes on three canvases. The children painted the portraits looking at the photos we had. It became a permanent three-part mural for the lobby forever reminding the kids of their achievement and enhancing the entrance to the sterile institutional old building.

In another elementary school, most of the children were first-generation Americans or immigrants from countries as widespread as China, Russia, and India. The sound of chatter in the halls combined at least three or four languages. Each participant in my group, from a home where English wasn't spoken, told a bit of their family history to the class. I asked them to describe what it felt like when they arrived in the US. By sharing their stories, the kids in the multicultural class saw that they had more in common than they thought. They chose the word "friendship." We created a seventeen-panel mural with the letters dancing like musical notes in the native languages and alphabets of the students. It hung as a frieze encircling the lobby, a welcome to all who entered the school.

Near Brooklyn wetlands, we made two seven-by-four-foot canvases flanking the school's auditorium stage. One depicted the fauna and land animals and the other the sea creatures found a few blocks away. The kids who couldn't sustain attention for long and needed instant gratification painted the backgrounds of water and grass. Those who loved detail work painted the fish, flowers, and plants.

I drew satisfaction from my artist residencies, making art a powerful tool of communication in communities that hadn't been aware of its value and had previously not incorporated it as part of their lives. I loved watching the increase of self-esteem in my young artists and grew attached to them. I yearned for a child of my own.

♋

AFTER A YEAR OF TRYING, I WASN'T PREGNANT, BUT WE WEREN'T worried, assuming it would happen. Bruce and I became closer, had sex more often, and at that point I looked at the process as a performance piece. It was fun.

Bruce's job of discovering new anti-aging products brought us to an oasis, Desert Hot Springs, to seek the Nature Doctor at the Miracle Manor, a fifties style motel, not restored, but reflecting over thirty years of use; it was a dive with a huge swimming pool that had steam rising. The Nature Doctor greeted us with casual warmth, clad in polyester pedal pushers and checked shirt. Beneath her perfect smooth skin and brown poufy country-western hairdo was a mature woman who appeared ageless and wise. "I'm Lois," she said. "Let me show you to your room. Why don't you get settled and then jump into the pool. That's where the miracles happen."

We unpacked, put on our bathing suits—in my case, a long-sleeved leotard—and headed toward the Olympic-sized pool, perfect for laps. I started my crawl stroke, but after a few times back and forth, the extreme heat of the water slowed me down. I floated for a while, the bright blue desert sky imprinted on the backs of my eyelids. Bruce was already in the adjoining whirlpool. I swam over to him and relaxed, staring at the snow on the surrounding Sierra Mountains.

Joining us, in her bikini, Lois said, "You two are basting perfectly. Let me tell you about the magic here. An aquifer, four hundred feet below the ground, is the source of the geothermal mineral water in the pools. There are therapeutic levels of sulfate, sodium, bicarbonate, and chloride. The swimming pool is 98°F. We are sitting in 104°F, but it's easy to soak up the warmth and minerals when you're not moving around."

She told us we looked like beets and suggested we jump into the cold pool then put on our robes and talk more about all the "good stuff" in her products. I let Bruce get to his business and lazily swam in the hot pool then cooled off in the cold. I couldn't get enough of the water, still on a mission to heal.

Back to soaking after his business conference, Bruce said, "Lois is also a psychic healer. She is offering to give you a free session to help you get pregnant." It sounded ridiculous, but the waters felt great. I was willing to see if there were any other powers at play.

The yellow room I entered in her wing of the motel had a serenity that was as enveloping as the desert heat. She asked me to lie down on a massage table, face up. I was surprised to see a wall of eight-by-ten-inch glossy black-and-white signed photos of show business celebrities attesting to her unnamed miracles. A large banner from Espirita Cristiana bearing Lois's name covered the opposite wall. The healing ceremony was brief. She hovered over me invoking the spirit Omra by repeating his name several times in a low guttural chant—OMRAOMRAOMRAOMRA—until it sounded like she was speaking in tongues. She professed to being his medium. It all seemed wacky, but I was there and curious to see where it would go. As her chant deepened and sounded more primal, she pulled my leg, informing me that it was a Filipino healing technique to balance me. I wanted to laugh but didn't. I wanted to believe. The funky room became enchanted with golden light after her invocation. I felt her loving, healing spirit, but I was happy when she said it was over. It was hard to take this seriously because of the hokeyness of the ceremony, the environment, and her country-western cowgirl appearance. But I did accept the rose quartz oblong pendant she placed around my neck to keep my heart open. I couldn't wait to tell Bruce about the session. I didn't think Omra would help get me pregnant, but we spent the night trying.

OUR DESIRE AND READINESS TO BE PARENTS REACHED ITS PEAK. The image of the child I had in the hospital bed, when I decided to live, needed to become a reality for me. I was ready to give a child the devotion my mother gave me; ready to imprint my love on a child's heart and my smile on her gaze; ready to care for a child the way my mother cared for me after the fire. I wanted to be that loving mother.

After every possible fertility test, the verdict was that we both had antibodies that resulted in my eggs rejecting Bruce's sperm! A friend of ours said that in many cultures this was grounds for leaving your husband. Yet my love for Bruce wasn't diminished; neither was my desire to have a family with him. In vitro fertilization wasn't an option because we didn't have enough money to try it more than once.

My friend David, who was HIV positive, had been telling me about an acupuncturist he was seeing who helped him to keep balanced and was prolonging his life.

"Dr. N is fabulous," he said. "I adore her. She's a beautiful strong Jewish woman who went to the best medical school and hospitals, got her MD, and then learned acupuncture by training in China. And she's a ballroom dancer. You want a baby? Go see her. She crosses all healing worlds and takes insurance."

I emerged from the R train at Thirty-Fourth Street and walked east on Thirty-Second Street, the block where Korean restaurants butted against each other. As I entered the elevator in the lobby, the scent of cooking oil and kimchee wrapped around me like a jungle of smells. When the elevator arrived on Dr. N's floor and I opened her door, incense replaced the food odors. The serene minimalist office with several well-placed large crystals transported me to calmness. The receptionist indicated I take a seat. A thin tall woman with a long crimson ponytail and silver high heels placing her over six feet tall glided over to me. With a beautiful smile, she shook my hand and introduced herself as Dr. N. I followed her to a little room separated from several other little rooms by fabric curtains. She instructed me to lie down on the narrow bed.

"Tell me why you're here," she said. Her blue eyes focused intensely on my face.

"I am having trouble getting pregnant. My husband and I each have antibodies that prevent fertilization. Can you help?"

"There are meridians I can work on that should balance out the antibodies and there's a good chance, especially if you keep your energy positive. Your husband should come in for treatment as well."

I was excited at the opportunity she offered and agreed.

I laid down on the table and she stuck needles in my forehead, ears, arms, feet, stomach. While she checked on the patients in the other cubicles, I meditated on harmony and having a baby, the thin needles exclamation points of my desire. Dr. N returned and removed them with a reassuring smile. Optimistic upon leaving, I had an image of every cell in my body vibrating with openness and fluidity and was too lightheaded to take the subway.

Bruce and I repeated this routine for months. I always felt cleansed or transformed in some way after each session but didn't get pregnant.

After a year of calculated sex, months of drinking stinky herbal teas for conception, fertility shots, and a round of artificial insemination, I continued to be barren. Our frustration fueled our determination to become parents. It became a single-minded goal. I was forty; neither of us thought the main reason to have a baby was the perpetuation of our genes. As cliché as it sounded to me, I didn't want to miss out on the experience of motherhood—nurturing a life, seeing the world from my child's perspective, providing a great environment for her to revel in its wonders. Our desire was to be a family.

My good friend and fellow artist, who I envied for her relationship with her son, told me over a martini that maybe I wasn't meant to be a parent and to view it as a blessing because my husband and I could enjoy life spontaneously. She was excited to be out having a drink with me, which she couldn't do whenever she felt like it but I could. She added wistfully that I would be able to put all the energy a child demands into my art. When I responded that she didn't understand the emptiness I felt, she confided about the anguish her twenty-year-old son was causing her. I saw her face transform to a tangle of tense lines and heard her voice raise its pitch teetering on panic.

I had always seen that dear friend as a super mom. Divorced for the last ten years, she had sole custody and worked hard supporting the boy on her own, while maintaining her painting practice. A talented artist, he also played chess, sang, wrote music, was charming, polite, and hip—just the kind of son I would want to have. I witnessed her encourage his strengths and envied their vacations to the Galapagos and Machu Picchu. The two of them operated as a team, cooking dinner together for Bruce and me several times.

I was shocked to hear that she no longer trusted her son and lived in fear of what he would or wouldn't do each day. She lowered her voice at our corner table in the back, telling me she was embarrassed to admit that the police arrested him on a minor charge, but she intervened and he did not go to jail. She was in debt paying an attorney and psychiatrists. She breathlessly told me how she had to hide her wallet at all times because her son's sneakiness was beyond recognition of the child she raised. She lived with distrust and over-vigilance that clearly was destroying her peace of mind. Her missing money turned up in the form of empty alcohol bottles buried under piles of dirty clothes in his room and customized metal pipes for smoking weed rattling in the washing machine, having fallen out of his jeans' pockets. She sighed that years of consequences and reward no longer meant anything to the young adult who was still her dependent and lived with her. His past achievements and engagement in school now gave way to just lying around his room. She didn't know what to do to help him and felt trapped and used.

I was horrified, speechless and at a loss of what to do for her. I thought this was an unusual, sad but temporary phase.

I also didn't hear any signals that if she had to do it again she would not be a mother. She was caught up in a situation that she couldn't control, but surely it would get better.

This wasn't the normal trajectory of child development. How could I take it as a cautionary tale? Nothing could diminish my own blind desire to be a mother. I couldn't see beyond a baby in my arms in the way any woman who longs for a child feels.

Bruce and I spent a weekend at a country inn with our friends Nancy and Simon and their four-year-old son, Alex, who was a miniature of the best qualities of each parent, her eyes and skin, his nose and mouth, the quick intelligence of both. It was clear how much attention and responsibility they joyfully directed toward their child. Walking on a trail, Alex pointed out orange salamanders scurrying into the brush and ran after them trying to catch one. When he did, we all looked at it with wonder. Simon, praising his son's swiftness and sharp eye, told him it was not his to keep and to gently put it down so the salamander could find its family, Alex's first lesson of capture and release. I picked up a few pine cones of different sizes and showed them to the boy. He ran around collecting more, screaming, "I have a tiny one, here's a skinny one, oh this one's fat." He brought them to Nancy to put in her bag. We all searched for interesting shapes and stuffed our pockets and backpacks. At the end of the trail, we arranged them in an intricate design resembling a pyramid in the middle of a mandala. Seeing the simplicity and complexity of nature through the boy's eyes was an extraordinary event. I loved their child and yearned for that challenge and its reward.

Our options for a biological child had run out since we didn't have the money or inclination for rounds of in vitro or surrogacy. After months of discussion and research, we decided that carrying on a bloodline wasn't as important for us as giving a baby who wouldn't have a chance for a good life the opportunity to have one. We went to a panel of adoption specialists who told us about the differences between open and closed adoptions, adopting through a lawyer, agencies that provided domestic adoptions and those that specialized in foreign ones. The foreign adoptions, where the children were most needy, sounded exactly like what we wanted to do. I asked questions about the policies of different countries. A man sitting behind me tapped me on the shoulder and said in a loud voice, "Do you want to adopt a foreign kid so you don't have to compete with the birth mother and the kid can't contact her?" I was astounded. I assumed the child was too much of a burden for the birth mother in a country where she could barely feed herself.

We believed that nurture was more important than nature. Devoting ourselves to the entirety of raising a child with our surplus of love was what we wanted. Adoption would be our course, and that baby would be ours like Nancy and Simon's son was theirs. Looking back, I see how naive we were to think it was as simple as that.

⟑

I LAY IN THE DARK UNABLE TO SLEEP AS BRUCE SNORED BESIDE ME. I heard friends' and a fellow art therapist's questions in my head. How can you raise a child whose family history is unknown? What if the birth mother took drugs, drank, and was malnourished during pregnancy? Sure babies and little kids are cute, but you could pour your love, time, and money into this person who might have genetic, physical, and emotional problems that are out of your control, someone who may be a huge disappointment to you because they are incapable of living up to your expectations. You don't know the potential problems that could manifest later in their life—jail, a mental institution. I was sure that happened as well to biological children of people who were not mentally ill or criminals. I didn't think our adopted child would be any more susceptible to these potential pitfalls.

I worked with hundreds of children in special education programs—autistic or developmentally disabled—and I got through to them. I saw their strengths beyond their disabilities. I saw the transformative power that making art with them produced and that was just for several hours of their lives in my classrooms and in hospitals where I worked as an art therapist, especially with Keisha whose first word at four years old was a color. A persistent voice in my brain resounded with the blind faith I had in the power of love, emotional and physical presence, and the environment to mold a human life to its fullest potential. I didn't believe there were any so-called defects I couldn't help fix, make right, or adjust to.

Yet by 4 a.m., the desolate hour when every little doubt became an overwhelming obstacle, I was still awake dwelling on the fragility of life, how the safety and well-being of a precious child was a parent's constant responsibility. I wondered how any parent could prevent something terrible from happening to their child especially when the child became more independent, and how much courage it took to assume that role. I would learn decades later the importance of that insight.

When I awoke to the day's brightness, nothing could diminish my own blind desire to be a mother. I thought about living in northern California a lifetime ago and remembered the feeling of a life growing inside me then and was happy to have had that sensation of fullness. I didn't regret the abortion, my chance for biological motherhood. I wasn't ready to be a mother then, didn't want the responsibility in my unstable life at twenty-five but was so ready now.

∾

OUR FIRST OPTION WAS ROMANIA, SINCE IT WAS THE BIRTHPLACE of my grandfather and had the world's eye on its orphanages brimming with babies who needed parents in 1990. We joined the legions of couples whose determination to raise a child became their main focus.

An agency specializing in Romanian adoptions vetted us, and a social worker pried into every aspect of our lives.

"What do you do when you are stressed?"

"Yoga," I answered.

"How much time do you spend together?"

"Every night and weekends."

"Do you have an extended family who will welcome the child?"

"Definitely."

"Please photograph pictures of your home and show the child's room."

We took pictures of our one-bedroom loft and indicated where we would build another room

The adoption agency connected us with a support group of parents seeking Romanian adoption. Irina, the orphanage's representative, came to New York to meet the prospective parents for the many needy babies. Each couple had her over for a meal to get to know each other. After dinner, we took her to the Museum of Modern Art to see a Brancusi exhibition. As one of my favorite

Romanian sculptors, I assumed she would enjoy the show and an evening at the Museum. A few months later on a Sunday morning, the phone rang. Interrupted from a dream, I answered.

"I have a healthy six-month-old boy for you," Irina said

Sitting on my bed I screamed, "A-h-h"

Bruce came running in, dripping from the shower. "What's wrong?" he said, staring at my tears and smile.

"Irina has a baby for us."

"Where? When?" Bruce screamed into the phone.

"I am here and can bring him to you but need $5,000 more in cash first."

"We've already paid $6,000. Is the extra money for the birth mother? We would be happy to help her," I said. We had a list of additional expenses yet to be paid to the agency to complete the adoption, and I didn't understand her request.

"You ask too many questions. I give him to someone else." She hung up.

We immediately called the Romanian-speaking person in the parent group who had assumed the leadership role and was host to Irina.

"We need to speak to Irina," Bruce said to him.

"She's not here," he replied.

"She just called us. She told us she had our baby, but then there were complications. Do you know what is going on? Do you know where she is?" Bruce asked.

"She doesn't want to talk to you and has gone out." He hung up. What an inappropriate response since we were part of a support group in which we shared an emotional vulnerability.

He had served as our connecting thread to potential happiness. The thread snapped. It was like being in a dingy on the ocean without oars or motor. We should have noticed the red flag sooner, but our desire for a baby blinded us.

"She probably went to sell the baby to someone else," Bruce said. The human being that was to complete our family had become a commodity. We were gullible and needy, then betrayed, disillusioned and deflated. We didn't see the levels of what was obviously a scam.

I called my friend Gail who I had met at an artist colony and told her the story. Her husband, Mort, a lawyer who worked for the Queens District Attorney said he would help us. Not only did we want our money back but wanted to protect anyone else who would be the next prey to Irina and her cohorts.

Bruce, restraining his anger and hurt, called back the man harboring the Romanian. "We need to meet with Irina. If she is not going to give us our baby, she has to return the money we have already given to her."

"She's flying out of JFK in a few hours."

"Listen schmuck, tell her I have a lawyer from the District Attorney's office with me and if she doesn't meet us and return the money, she will never be allowed in this country again, at the least. I have a feeling that you are in for a little trouble yourself. We will be at your house in half an hour."

Above the clunking hum of the air conditioner cooling our loft from the sweltering heat of the late June day, I heard the screech of tires outside our window as Bruce began his drive to Brooklyn. He was to pick up the lawyer and go to the house, which in the past had been the meeting place for commiserating childless couples.

While waiting for the outcome of the mission, I called my mother and told her everything that happened. I could always depend on her for consolation.

"If it's meant to be it will be," she said. Then I just sat staring at the phone waiting for it to ring. Two hours later Bruce called. Out of breath and excited he said, "Brahna, it was like an episode of *Law and Order*."

"Are you OK? Details, please."

"I'm great. Mort was brilliant. I've gotta tell you the story. We rang the bell and when the guy answered the door after a minute or two, we saw Irina running out the back. She was carrying the bundle I assumed was the baby. We ran after her. My marathon training came in handy. I was right on her tail as she climbed the stairs to the roof and went up there after her. What was I supposed to do? I cornered her. She held the bundle close to her throbbing chest. I could feel and hear my own heart pumping. I just stared at her afraid to reach for the baby. I heard Mort and her conspirator coming up the stairs. My head was spinning, not knowing what to expect. What if he or Irina had a gun? We were all on the silver painted tar roof, sweating like crazy, the sun blinding us."

"Wow. Was she going to jump off the four-story roof to escape?"

"No. She dangled the baby over the parapet of the roof as a hostage, saying she would drop him over the side if we didn't let her go. But the blanket started unraveling, and it was apparent it was just lumped up rags. Mort told the translator that she obviously wasn't holding a baby and to tell her if she didn't give us the $6,000, she would be arrested for fraud and have her visa revoked just for starters.

"Standing on the edge of the roof, Irina looked like our cat after she's sneaked a piece of food from the table and we'd cornered her. Then she shrugged, dropped the bundle of rags and pulled out the cash from a fabric pouch she had hidden between her breasts under her blouse. She clutched the pouch.

"'You have to promise that since she is giving back the money, you will leave us all alone,' her translator said.

"'The only promise I will make is that you will have more trouble than you can imagine if she doesn't return it,' Mort replied.

"He was so cool. She held out the money. I asked him to take it from her. Touching something intimately tucked in her body revolted me. Now I have the cash and am in an air-conditioned diner with Mort having a cold drink and a bite. He's going to press charges this week so no one else gets scammed. See you soon. I love you so much."

I was relieved they had gotten the money back and proud of my husband's courageousness. However, by the time he came home my hopes for a child had careened faster downhill than an Olympic skier on a perfectly packed slope. We had been so desperate that we didn't pay enough attention to the little things in the process that didn't make sense. In hindsight, we really didn't know much about the guy in Brooklyn.

∽

I WAS TIRED OF PUTTING OUR LIFE ON HOLD UNTIL WE HAD A BABY, tired of it being the focus of our existence. I just wanted to chill in our little country house to relieve the stress. If we were meant to be parents, we would; if not, at least we had the house, and I would have a permanent studio in nature. I decided to focus on my work there and spend all summers and time off with Bruce instead of on a baby mission. I wanted to create something with him, and if it couldn't be a baby, then the home in the country would do. I don't think I was the first woman to have this thought. We hired a local builder to construct a deck on which to eat outdoors, and hung Sheetrock to make three rooms in the basement, including Bruce's office entered through glass doors that provided a sweeping view of the pond. I made a trade with an architect friend—I gave him a painting, and he drew plans for my studio; a local carpenter built it.

If I had not turned my hands and mind to making art, I wouldn't have been able to function. I expanded my painting focus toward the public arena. The projects I was doing in schools solidified my belief that art didn't necessarily have to exist only in the rarefied world of museums and galleries. I wanted to make art that integrated into people's everyday lives. I started entering painting competitions for public spaces. This was an arduous process and the chances of me being rewarded for selection were about the same as finding a child that was destined to be ours. It was in that studio, in addition to the Jimmy paintings, that I conceived of and executed a small painting for my entry to a competition sponsored by the New York City Department of Health's anti-smoking campaign. I painted two figures facing each other in profile, their heads filling most of the canvas. The black woman had an uncompromising wide-eyed stare and wore a pale blue surgical mask that covered her nose and mouth. The tan-skinned man, who resembled handsome Raoul Julia, stared at her aggressively, his mouth snarling and exhaling smoke. A cigarette in his hand pointed in her direction. Overlapping smoke rings filled in the background.

I was one of a handful of artists chosen to enlarge their painting into mural size. My assigned location was a brick wall on the side of an apartment building facing the open expanse of an empty lot in the South Bronx. I was thrilled—a big grin on my face in a photograph taken at City Hall awarding the artists their projects. I loved working on scaffolding with my assistant, reproducing my own art. The thrill of painting ten feet off the ground while listening to my rhythm and blues cassettes blaring from my boom box was my idea of flying. I had painted stage sets eleven years earlier, but this mural was more than twice as big. For the first time since the fire ten years before, the summer heat played a secondary role in affecting my day-to-day life. I was in heaven wearing paint-splattered clothes. I remained in that exalted state for about a month until the mural's completion.

∽

DURING OUR BABY HUNT HIATUS, JIMMY DIED. AFTER GOING TO the cemetery, we sat in my parents' living room, the house sagging with sadness. Surrounded by platters of smoked fish, bagels, and distant relatives and friends, I looked around and realized that with Jimmy's absence, our immediate family was so small that the subtraction of him lessened it exponentially, creating a lack of solidity. When the people left and just Bruce, my parents, and I remained, "We need to adopt a baby," fell out of my mouth. My grief had amplified my desperation.

Not long afterward, we began our search again. This time we tried a domestic adoption agency. They matched would-be parents with young women who had contacted the agency because they didn't want to or weren't in a position to keep their babies. These young women chose of which couple they wanted to adopt their baby. Brittany in Texarkana picked us after reading our information and our letter about giving a child a supportive, creative, and loving home. During our phone interviews, she charmed us with her sweetness and earnestness in wanting to find the best environment and family. We couldn't wait to meet her and in the meantime, we agreed to pay her bills while she was pregnant. We wanted her to receive good pre-natal care and healthy food.

During one of my rare weeding sessions in my flailing flower garden upstate, the phone rang.

I ran into the house to answer it and brought the cordless device outside to talk, relieved to have something else to do while extracting unwanted roots. I hoped that my sparse garden didn't reflect anything more than my disinterest in always tending to it. I sat in the dirt bed in front of the house, small spade in one hand, phone in the other. It was Brittany.

"How are you feeling?" I asked, pleased to hear her voice.

"I'm starting to get real big and don't want to do anything but hang out and watch my soaps and eat Doritos," she said. "What are you all doing?"

"Just weeding the flowerbed."

"Oh, I like that. My baby will have pretty flowers to look at." I hoped so.

I began loving my sparse garden.

"My mom is always nagging me. You have such a nice voice. I know you'll be a great mama for my baby."

"Thanks. I'll try my hardest. She'll have lots of love."

"Yeah. Well, I just wanted to say hi and thank you for the money for the doctor and food."

The next time she called, I was out in the garden again planting salvia, purple irises, and alum.

She was crying.

"What's the matter, Brittany? Are you OK? How's the baby?"

"I'm fat as a house and the baby is fine. She'll be here in a week or so. I saw the sonogram today." She paused. I held my breath.

"Please don't hate me, but I want to keep her. She's mine. She's my flesh and blood. I hope you get a baby someday soon. You deserve one." She hung up before I could say anything.

Why were we repeatedly putting ourselves through this? We had already been promised then denied a baby from Bulgaria and Kiev, as well. I had been in the basement laundry room with the single light bulb when we received those disappointments.

I ran to the vegetable garden. The hell with the flowers. Bruce, shirtless, clad in shorts and gardening vest, pockets bulging with seed packets and tools, was digging with a hoe. The sweat shined on his tanned arms and his forehead beneath his baseball cap.

"That's it. I've had it. Brittany is keeping the baby. We're just being masochists. Forget about us being parents. I'm done."

He held me silently, nodding. Our social worker's evaluation of us was about to expire.

The summer was at its height of heat, and I was relieved to spend the rest of it at our house upstate. We invited friends from the city. One weekend, Judy, with her sweet and musically talented seven-year-old daughter, and Nancy and Simon, with their adorable precocious Alex, who was now nine, were guests. I didn't realize until we were having lunch and both mothers were commiserating about not having enough time to themselves, how jealous I was.

"You should be grateful you have a child," I snapped at both of them. "Stop kvetching. You're luckier than you know."

They stared at me at first in silence, then Judy said, "We're just talking about our lives, like you talk about yours. Hey, it's not about what we have and you don't. You have this house."

I apologized under my breath, not being able to face them and went outside for a long walk down a country road. Not only was I irredeemably embarrassed at my outburst but still felt deprived because becoming parents had happened so naturally and easily for them.

When I returned, I took Bruce aside and said, "Let's call Sue, the social worker, and renew our evaluation. I really want a child."

Every time I got discouraged and felt I couldn't spend my life trying to be a mother and I was grateful to have my husband, my art, our house, I was suppressing the fact that I really wanted to be a mother. If I isolated myself in the world I created, that desire could stay hidden. Yet it didn't take much to dig it up. Being with my close friends, who had big careers but whose lives had greater dimension with their children, made my need to experience motherhood full-blown. We had watched every phase of Alex's nine-year-old life, and I wanted that experience firsthand day to day.

"OK. We can call Sue on Monday," he said.

"Why not now?" I said. "It's Saturday afternoon. If she's home in the city, she might want to drive up here for a day in the country out of the heat. She did say that she wanted to see the house for the follow-up evaluation."

"Are you nuts? We have guests and I'm sure she has her own plans."

"She'll see that we hang out with friends with kids. It's good. Can you ple-e-e-e-ase call her?"

Sue the social worker showed up the next day. Judy and I were swimming in the pond. Nestled next to wild blueberry bushes, everyone else lounged on a blanket made lumpy by the field of over grown wild flowers beneath it. We heard Sue's car pull up. She got out, stretched, took a deep breath, and exhaled loudly enough for all of us to hear. She preferred the blanket to the pond. Bruce, the perfect host, served cold juice and a picnic lunch. I joined them. After finishing the meal, I gave her the grand tour, especially pointing out the room in the basement with the window, closet, and en suite bath, which would be the baby's room. Currently it had our guests' clothes and their boy's toys scattered on the beige tweed rug.

Bruce and I sat with Sue under the white market umbrella at the round, wooden table on our deck. We updated her about our lives. I heard the shouts of the kids playing below us on the grass and noticed their parents lazily look up every now and then for safety checks before returning to their Sunday *New York Times*. Depression overcame me. Sue was making sure we were fit to be parents, filling out official forms that covered our table. She was analyzing and judging our life. My friends never had to go through this.

"We've had so many disappointments, I'm not really sure I want to continue," I told Sue.

"I have a really good lead for you. There's an agency in Minnesota that is looking for homes to place Paraguayan babies. Paraguay has only been open for adoption for less than a year because an elected official replaced the dictator. The average family has thirteen kids, and it is a terribly poor country. Instead of abandoning their unwanted babies, now mothers can put them in small foster homes, hoping families will adopt them and know that at least caretakers will feed and shelter their infants until that happens. This agency has pictures of infants who desperately need homes. It can't hurt to contact them and look. I've heard the success rate is super high."

"OK. I'll contact her. Thanks," I said. I felt skeptical and considering a new continent pointed to our desperation.

We also were running low on money. I hunted through my jewelry box, the one that had trinkets from pre-fire boyfriends. I found strands of surrealist necklaces made by Billy, one of green plastic Barbie Doll combs looked almost tribal. It was cool, but no monetary value there.

A dancing prism of light skipped along the side of the box. The reflection was from the diamond ring Jake had given me. It was buried in the part of my mind labeled past. I had forgotten about its brilliance. I had it appraised and found that the value should be able to cover most of the costs of this adoption. I thought of the image I had in the burn unit of Jake holding the hand of a small child. I told Bruce we had this covered and contacted the agency in Minnesota.

15

THE PACKAGE

ABOUT A WEEK LATER, A PACKAGE ARRIVED IN OUR mailbox from the adoption agency. Rushing into Bruce's office, I flung it on his desk in front of him and we ripped it open. The faces of over a dozen sweet baby boys stared at us. I had always imagined raising a daughter, but here were irresistible infants who had no parents. Our original incentive to adopt lay before us. We leafed through the pages and at the same time pointed to a small baby with slightly slanted eyes, rosy cheeks, sparse blondish hair, and an impish toothless grin. His smile looked like my brother's in his 1951 baby picture. "That's our son," we said in unison. "We'll name him after Jimmy."

I knew that this baby in the photo was meant to be ours. A little bit of my brother had reappeared. I immediately called the agency and told her we wanted to adopt him.

"It's a four month process from the time you identify the baby to completing the paperwork in Paraguay. Although the baby is in a small orphanage, the birth mother has to be contacted again to make sure she hasn't changed her mind," said Deb, the agency owner.

"Do mothers change their minds often?"

"Never. They give up the babies at birth because they just can't take care of another child. This particular mother never even saw her baby. She is relieved that he is being cared for in the orphanage."

I pointed out that I wanted to go to Paraguay immediately just to see him, to make sure he was real, to make sure he was healthy. We could wait to start the paperwork, but I wanted to know this boy from the earliest possible moment in his life.

Deb told us that no one traveled to Paraguay for a sneak peek before the process began because they had to leave the baby there.

However, if I really wanted to make the trip, she would check with the lawyer, Maria, to see if it was feasible. If so, Maria would meet us at the hotel and bring the baby to stay with us there for a week. It would be an unofficial visit. The proceedings couldn't start for another four months, and we were not guaranteed this child until all the papers were stamped and signed by the government. She asked again if we were certain we really wanted to go now since we would need to return in a few months to sign the papers anyway.

None of this deterred me. Paraguay suddenly felt very close, and a few months felt like an eternity. I wanted to hold the infant now. Bruce wondered if we could be setting ourselves up for disappointment again. He said it was crazy to go on an unofficial visit with no guarantee. His blue eyes opened so large they looked like a piece of sky had fallen and landed below his brow, displaying an expression of fear and nervousness, with which I had become familiar.

I was adamant that this time was different. We had never seen a picture of the baby we were going to adopt before. We knew he existed and was definitely the one. How could we not take this trip?

Although to someone else my reaction could have seemed irrational, Bruce understood. We made phone calls to doctors and a child psychiatrist friend to ask what we should be observing. We had no idea about "our" baby or his environment. We soon found out that his birth mother was a thirty-year-old seamstress. She had several other sons and a hard time feeding and caring for them.

A few weeks later, we arrived at El Gran Hotel de Paraguay in a peaceful residential neighborhood where diplomats lived, away from the center of Asuncion, the capital city. The funky, rambling, one-story colonial mansion had been built in the late 1800s or early 1900s by a former dictator as a home for his mistress. Germans fleeing their country after WWII had bought it and converted it to a finca-style hotel. The modest rooms with dark-shuttered windows and heavy colonial ebony furniture opened into courtyards with monkeys and parrots in cages. This was not a modern high-end, hi-rise hotel; it was very South American, historic, and comfortably homey.

We sat in the lobby on one of the overstuffed leather sofas gathered around a big wooden coffee table, our backs to the patio with mango trees so full of fruit we could hear the ripe ones dropping on the ground. Our eyes didn't waver from the large wooden entrance door, waiting to meet Maria the attorney and our baby, our hands locked in each other's with anticipation.

After what seemed like hours, Maria and an interpreter arrived with a baby boy. In the hotel lobby, I shook her hand and anxiously held my arms out as she handed the baby to me. I had studied his photo so often that every detail of his image imprinted itself in my brain. I already thought of him as ours and inexplicably knew on a core level that we were destined to be his parents. I looked down at the infant with jet black hair and long skinny body and realized he was the wrong one.

I hadn't felt tired after the seventeen-hour flight buoyed by the anticipation of holding our son. Now my adrenaline pumped to fight despair. Was this yet another slap in the face by parenthood that had never attached itself to us? Was it the cruelest ruse of all? Did they take us for fools thinking we wouldn't notice because all babies were interchangeable? Was our baby still alive and available? Was this really happening? I would not let it happen. It usually took me a day or two in a Spanish-speaking country to sound fluent. At that moment, Spanish spewed out of my mouth, bombarding the air of the hotel lobby.

"This is not our baby," I said to Maria, bypassing the interpreter. "Please take us to him."

"It's already night time and you are not allowed in the orphanage. I will bring him tomorrow."

"No," I pleaded. "We have such a short time here we need to be with him tonight. Please take us. You have to go back to return this baby anyway."

Perhaps it was because I spoke Spanish or my earnest insistence or the fact she had made a mistake, but Maria agreed to take us with her to the orphanage. We left the city in a matter of minutes and traveled on bumpy dirt roads without streetlights. The car's headlights guided us through the blanket of darkness until we stopped at a cottage on the side of the road without sidewalks. Inside the one-room house crammed with twenty cribs, babies stared up at ceiling fans. The only caretakers present were a couple of twelve-year-old girls who picked up crying infants and changed them on a table that was a running track for cockroaches. We spotted him immediately. He was looking at the fan and smiling. One of the girls changed his diaper, and we were on our way back to the hotel.

I finally had my baby in my arms. Sitting in the back seat of the car, jostling along in the dark, I blindly trusted the driver would deliver us to the hotel. All I cared about was the bundle of life I dearly held so close to my chest that my heartbeat and his drowned out the car's engine. The smell of my sweaty infant was sweeter than that of the wild jasmine lining the dusty road.

For years, I had been eyeing baby clothes, an aspiration of something I would need someday. Before setting out on the trip to Paraguay, I indulged in a few miniature cotton items. Back in the hotel room I removed the polyester onesie patterned with soccer balls and let our baby's body breathe in a little cotton tee shirt and diaper. It was one of the minor acts I performed on that trip staking claim to him, changing him from an orphan to our son.

Bruce and I spent the next week blissfully tired, with our baby, Jaime, named for my brother. When he cried, one of us took him out of the room and sat on the low stone wall separating the hotel rooms from the monkey and bird cages, cradling and humming to Jaime while he drifted off to the squawks and caws. We quickly learned how and when to change diapers and feed him formula. The breezes through the palm trees lulled us as Jaime and I lay on our stomachs on a blue blanket on the grass in the shade next to the hotel swimming pool while Bruce catnapped. We had to keep a low profile, watching our words with the other guests. This trip was off the official radar. We happily became a world of three.

One day we took Jaime on a guided tour of Paraguay, hoping it would serve as a subliminal memory of his roots and an adventure we could recall with him in the future, but we would wait a while to tell him that the national dance involved young women balancing a pyramid of wine bottles on their heads. A little overzealous, wanting to expose him to art as soon as possible, we took him to his first museum, Museo Del Barro, which had Guarani art and rooms lined with masks. In retrospect, I was overly eager in assuming that my four-month-old infant with Guarani eyes would connect on a deep level with the art of his partial ancestry. I wanted to immerse him in his native culture but was doing so as a tourist without realizing it. Seated in a lightweight stroller borrowed from Judy, I pushed him through the narrow cobblestone streets of our hotel's residential neighborhood. As Jaime bounced in his seat, I felt like I was walking on hot rocks, my thin-soled sandals a flimsy barrier to the rising heat. We brought him to Dr. Frutos who declared him healthy, his engaging smile a survival skill he had already learned at this tender age. We couldn't have been happier, until the day we had to leave.

I was in the shower when Bruce came into the bathroom and said the woman had come to take Jaime back to the orphanage. I ran out of the bathroom dripping, wrapped in a towel to see her walking out the door with him. "Wait," I screamed and insisted on hugging my son and covering him with kisses before they left. His formula and powder smell and the silky fuzz of his hair on my cheek stayed with me for the next three months.

Back in New York, I told myself that our baby was in Paraguay, and we would all be together soon. Since it took months to complete adoption papers and give the birth mother a chance to change her mind, Jaime consumed my thoughts. Coming out of an East Village restaurant, I approached a couple wheeling an infant and asked if their baby was four months old. When they said yes, I told them we had a son that age too. Bruce squeezed my hand. Was it in confirmation or to keep me from engaging with them any further? I never knew. In my mind, I was like them, no longer childless. Part of me thought I was too obsessed and maybe delusional. However, my bite-sized taste of motherhood was so delicious I couldn't bear to think it wouldn't be an on-going feast.

Two and a half months later, we felt like we were returning home when we arrived at El Gran Hotel de Paraguay. Maria brought Jaime to us immediately. Our documents had been prepared. The owner of the hotel handed him a bottle filled with fresh-squeezed carrot juice. We joined the instant community of the other guests with their infants and toddlers waiting for the government signing of endless papers. We gathered information on the details of the process from those who were there longer. Bruce supplemented huge breakfasts of eggs and potatoes by catching ripe mangoes in the air as they dropped off the trees. When he peeled them, the pulpy flesh sensuously dripped from his fingers.

We formed a carriage brigade with other parents and their soon-to-be adopted babies. Wheeling the bumping strollers over uneven sidewalks, we explored the labyrinthine alleys of the markets in downtown Asuncion, amidst decaying old buildings. Alongside woven baskets and fabrics, beautiful women balanced sugar-coated pastries in reed baskets on their shoulders, a veil of flies swarming around them. Dozens of barefoot, thin, dirty children sold bottle caps for guarani, Paraguayan coins. Our babies in their strollers were clean and cherished, but what about these other children?

At night a live Paraguayan band played in the dining room decorated with hand-painted verdant vines and local foliage on the walls and ceiling. We marched to the music into dinner as part of a processional, along with the owners, their friends, and other guests. Bruce, Jaime, and I sat with Timothy and his soon-to-be adopted two-and-a-half-year-old, Abie. I had never experienced anything like these musical dinners and videotaped them, zooming in on members of the owners' family sitting smugly in the corner in their Teutonic splendor.

"You are so outrageous filming those people. They'll take away your camera. I think they are trying to be incognito. I'm sure they're ex-Nazis," whispered Timothy. We were all drunk on baby love seated at our round table with our little ones strapped into wicker chairs for lack of high chairs. "I want a copy of the cassette," he whispered conspiratorially.

We took turns piling our plates from the Paraguayan buffet: fresh local meats roasted on a grill outside under a canopy on the patio and my favorite—the spicy corn bread with cheese and onion. Although not a meat eater, the abundance was impressive. The Paraguayan harp with its haunting sound dominated the evening. Learning that the Guarani, the predominant indigenous people of the country, were extremely musical, I brought Jaime up to the harp player to hear and see the instrument. He responded by gurgling, smiling, and wiggling in my arms. Like many new mothers, I was convinced he had musical talent, which as he grew older proved to be true. Surrounding him with his native music made me feel like I was being a good mother.

It took two weeks for us to obtain and sign the reams of papers from different government agencies. Bruce then returned to New York to make sure the room the contractor was building for Jaime would be ready. My loft was going through yet another transformation since the fire.

I spent over a week alone with my baby. I took him to have fingerprints, his tiny fingers smudged with ink. I worried he would put them in his mouth and wondered what to do about it, but he was distracted by a fish tank that filled half the room. I waited for days for the fingerprints to be recorded, waited to receive government stamps, and waited for Jaime's passport and everything else not in my control to be completed. Mothering didn't seem very hard. I was infatuated. He filled my heart.

By the end of February 1993, everything was completed. I had permission to take Jaime home. On the seventeen-hour plane ride, I got my first taste of multitasking as a mom, trying to balance my food tray and my crying baby on my lap during the bumpy flight. I was petrified of either bumping his head or burning it with hot food and knew he needed to be changed. I wanted to transform myself into Krishna with hands to spare.

At JFK, as I wheeled our son in his lightweight stroller out of customs, my parents and Bruce formed a wall of welcoming warmth—crying, cooing, and laughing, their arms laden with wool blankets, booties, hats, and mittens, all crocheted by my mother. The new member of our family was about to experience his first frigid temperatures.

On February 26, 1993, Jaime's first day in his new home in Tribeca, I dressed him in a thick, cotton-ribbed, sunflower yellow onesie. His tiny room had two large windows on the brick western wall facing the Hudson. I twirled prisms I had just hung with clear fishing line. He followed the shifting rainbows with his eyes, trying to catch them in his hands, mouth open in delight. A news flash interrupted the classical music on the radio: *A truck bomb detonated below the north tower of the World Trade Center. Many people are injured. There is underground damage but all is under control. The damage is contained. No reason to panic.*

My brain registered the terrible news. However, although the World Trade Center was only a few blocks away, I felt no threat, just a freak accident I thought. It was inconceivable to me that anything bad could happen to us on that day. We were in a protective bubble. My whole universe was love in a yellow onesie.

It had been eleven years since I was burned in that same loft. Jaime's room had been part of my studio. I was still there, now an artist, mother, wife, activist, swimmer, and very much alive.

EPILOGUE

ALTHOUGH BEING BURNED WAS A DEFINING MOMENT OF my life, it doesn't define who I am but informs who I've become. Decades later, the trauma of the fire is still part of me, tucked away as is the nature of trauma. Triggered by a memory of the event, sometimes a blazing bonfire or when something bad happens that is beyond my control, my immediate response is helplessness. Yet within a few minutes, I realize that I can handle and accept whatever situation presents itself. I figure out a solution and act upon it.

∽

THIRTY-TWO YEARS AFTER THE FIRE I MOVED TO BROOKLYN Heights. Much of my life had changed except my swimming ritual. I chose to live across the street from an indoor pool at a Y, so I could easily engage in the sublime act of submersion and keep my body balanced and fluid.

Although there are disadvantages to a pool compared to nature's open distances, I appreciated the lack of undertow, yearlong accessibility, and unlikelihood of drowning.

I tried to swim at 9:30 a.m. every day, before family time and just after the aquatic rush hour. Leisurely, I glided at a continual slow and steady pace until I swam half a mile. Around my tenth lap, I felt my mind's grip loosen on whatever was nagging me. Solutions to problems came and went, as did the problems—each with equal weightlessness.

∽

I WAS THE ONLY ONE CHANGING IN THE LOCKER ROOM AFTER MY swim. A woman entered. She approached me in my nakedness, ran her finger down my arm, breaching my physical boundary. She said in an indistinguishable accent, "What happened to this?"

"I was burned," I automatically answered. I didn't consider any alternative response to the question asked countless times over thirty years and always hated the attention and wanted to halt it.

She stood there for another minute, then said, "We never know what will happen do we? But you have a normal life?"

"Yes," I replied. I wondered what normal was, but knew I'd worked hard to make the life I had. I breathed a sigh of relief as she left, and I finished putting on my clothes.

∽

WHEN JAIME WAS SEVEN, I NEEDED MORE INCOME TO INFUSE INTO our family. Bruce was struggling with his business, and I became a real estate broker. Yet I never gave up my art or being home every night to make dinner for my son. I learned to use the left side of my brain and sometimes made serious money. I enjoyed and cherished my clients, being a reassuring sounding board for emotions induced by change and guiding them into another phase of their life in a new home. I also loved walking through fabulous New York spaces seeing spectacular architectural details and views not visible from the street.

My former upstairs Tribeca neighbor hired me to sell her loft on the third floor. She bought it in the nineties when I lived on the second floor. I had moved to this then-warehouse in 1979 as a young painter with a burgeoning career and lived there for twenty-seven years. Our small four-unit building entwined its occupants as shareholders, creating an intimate knowledge of each other's habits and relationships. My neighbor, now client, used to climb through my window onto the fire escape to reach her loft when she forgot her key.

Although I no longer lived in the building, having sold my loft, I had a strong attachment to the bricks ingrained with the memories of my painting success, the devastating accident, my marriage, and my son's first thirteen years. As part of the first wave of owners, and having sold two lofts there, I was the real estate expert.

While staging her home, my client camped out in what used to be my loft, with the current absentee owners' permission. She asked me to meet her there, not knowing the details or location of the fire. I hadn't been inside since I sold it. My breath shortened when the elevator door opened onto the second floor. Was I ready to encounter remnants of my past?

I searched the corner near the entry door for the small ebony mark burnished into the oak floor from a flying spark the day I became a human torch. It was erased by the sanded, polished floors. The new state-of-the-art kitchen in what had been my studio space, the bedroom pod, sleek wood cabinetry, and central air no longer contained any sign of my past. My life and reason to be in the building had changed. The river view was the same, but I felt as newly configured as the space.

I found buyers for my neighbor's loft. Without a building manager to provide the lawyers with necessary papers, I needed to excavate them from the locked file cabinet on the second floor landing.

The hallway still had the dusty gray concrete floor. I heard faint echoes of my screams when I was ablaze, the shrill of sirens, the firefighters' heavy thumping, and the creaking of a stretcher taking me down the stairs.

I focused on the task of finding the building documents. I opened the two stuffed drawers. Overwhelmed, I piled dozens of folders on top of the cabinet and lined the rest along the floor.

Files labeled in my mother's perfect cursive hand and her clear signature on building mortgages and agreements blind-sided me. Thirty-six years before, my neighbors and I, absorbed in our art and youth, had no interest in record keeping. My mom, Paula, with outstanding organizational skills, took on that responsibility.

I froze holding the unexpected reminders of my late mother. I envisioned her wearing one of her hand-made crocheted sweaters. I still missed her intensely and missed not being able to call her.

Staring at the documents in the hallway, I remembered her herding us shareholders to take care of business.

My mother's ghostly presence renewed my awareness of her support that bolstered and aided me.

Now I was the one helping people move forward with their lives. Tackling the piles of papers, I looked at my hands, scarred and wrinkled, sifting through every folder as if on a treasure hunt. With each discovery of a relevant document, I hissed a triumphant "YES!" my head and the landing reverberating with the fresh sound clearing the haunted air. In part, I had become my mother—the problem solver, the organizer, the one people counted on to make sure everything went smoothly. I found the papers I needed and with renewed strength left the cabinet key in my client's loft, took the elevator to the lobby and walked out the front door, leaving behind the site of the fire and its damage.

WHEN HURRICANE SANDY SWOOPED THROUGH MANHATTAN BEACH in 2012, it blew out the walls and flooded my parents' dream home, where I had recuperated thirty years before. Most of the neighbors sold their homes. My father, recently widowed at ninety-one, insisted he would live the rest of his life in his house, imprinted with his sixty-two-year marriage to my mother, who had passed three years before.

After repairs, he moved back. Dressed in jeans and flannel shirt, hardly making a dent in the cushion of his love seat in the den, Dad waited for me. Photographs of four generations of our family covered the walls, my father, my son, and I the only ones left. Sometimes we went upstairs to the terrace and sat on dilapidated plastic chairs eating hummus and drinking seltzer, smelling the ocean, watching the gentle breeze through the trees while the cement mixer next door noisily filled the new neighbor's front yard.

His bi-weekly messenger from the outside world, I told him about my day, knowing he was the only one who cared since my divorce. He listened with full attention. "I'm sorry I never talked to you about your work or art, but I don't know anything about it. Painting is a mystery to me, and you know I don't like to appear unknowledgeable. But baby, I've always been so proud of you," he said. "I adore you." Tears welled up, finally feeling that after sixty years he saw me.

During his last year, I visited him several times a week. He fiercely wanted control of his life. Yet I became my mother taking charge. He repeated stories. "When I had no money and started out," he said, "a customer took your mother and me for our first lobster dinner. We grew up kosher. What did we know from shellfish? Your mother loved lobster. I loved seeing her happy." We both missed her, and for the first time we held each other and cried. I placed my palm up to his. We had the same long, graceful fingers. Stroking his hand covered with spreading age spots and surfaced veins, I said, "I'm here as long as you want me to be. Don't worry about me and my boy. Just know that when you leave us, you'll be with Mommy again." He stopped breathing and was gone.

DR. JANE HAHER, WHO SAVED MY ARM AND GAVE ME ENORMOUS encouragement to paint again, became the head of St. Vincent's Reconstructive and Plastic Surgery Department. Real estate developers bought the hospital and turned it into expensive condominiums in the 2010s. During the years that Dr. Haher had been in my life, she invited my mother and me to her apartment near her office on the Upper East Side. When I started writing this book, I wanted to talk to her. I went to her office, and they told me she had sold her practice. I went to her apartment building, and they said she had moved. I checked the internet and couldn't find any way to contact her for years. Recently, I found a website saying she volunteered at a clinic in New Mexico and another with her picture, rebranding herself as an artist. She is a very prolific painter living in Santa Fe. Her paintings are beautiful, colorful, and masterful. She is following the passion she wanted me to resume for myself.

～

My marriage to Bruce lasted eighteen years. I was right about him being a generous, kind man. However, I became stronger and more self-confident and needed more than just kindness in a partner. Our lifestyles seemed irreconcilable, and we didn't speak for over ten years.

Recently, we became friends when I needed him to be involved with Jaime. Our son's series of can-you-believe-what-he's-doing-now moments became our initial new bond. Bruce and I are on speed dial and each other's emergency contact person. The summer I emptied my parents' house of four generations of objects, clothes, and memories, including photos of our wedding, Bruce was there with me helping to sort and bag the four thousand square feet, room by room.

It took me thirty years to be able to buy a small modest house in the Springs, where I became a swimmer and much of my restoration from the fire took place. Three years later, alone in my little house surrounded by trees, I was on a step stool working on a painting. I lost my balance and fell. I couldn't budge. From the floor, I yanked at the chord charging my cell phone on the counter and instinctively called Bruce. "Help me. I need you. I am here alaone." One hundred miles away, he said, "call 911."

After cat scans and x-rays in the hospital, the diagnosis was a broken neck. "Don't move," the resident doctor told me. "You could be paralyzed for life." Petrified, my brain flew in every direction, including pulling my own plug. A few hours later, secure in a bulky neck brace after my body responded to taps and strokes, he reassured me I wouldn't be paralyzed and a specialist in the city should determine the need for surgery. Meanwhile, in the trauma unit for over a week, I couldn't move my head, unable to turn, look up or down. The pain shooting through my skull and neck was unbearable.

Terrified of not having control of my body and my life, let alone plan for anything in my future, was a blow of another life-altering accident that tested my mental grit. I wasn't sure my will was strong enough to recover in isolation.

When discharged from the hospital, I returned to my house to gather my things. I knew it was impossible to be there alone. My injuries prevented functioning, including driving.

Bruce took the first train out. He told me that calling him after the fall was a turning point in his life, a commitment to help me heal. It was an eerie recollection of our past.

Although being divorced absolved our vows, he was there in sickness as I would be for him eventually. Yet Bruce said, "I have my own life but will stay with you for a month." When he drove off to do errands, I counted the minutes before his return, unsure if missing him or the fear of being alone was stronger. He wanted to be there for me, the woman he loved, as the more confident and honest man he had become since the divorce. Laying on L-shaped single beds head to toe in the downstairs guest room, filled with light and verdant views, he read D. H. Lawrence's *Women in Love* out loud until one of us drifted off. For the first time in years, I felt safe, swathed in protection.

Upon returning to the city, I found a spine specialist who fused the first three vertebrae closest to my brain. He delivered the bad news that I may not be able to swim in open water ever again and had to wear a brace for an additional six months.

My son said he wanted to take care of me but knew he couldn't do all the things I needed. Bruce, a natural caretaker, stepped up, binding us in a new yet familiar way. However, we didn't make future plans.

When the pandemic struck, six months after breaking my neck, Bruce, still there, moved in so he wouldn't have to take the subway between his apartment and mine. My ex and I were not a couple, rather a couple of dear friends riding out a world disaster together. After years of living alone, his presence in my apartment, even when he was in another room, felt intimate. In order to sleep, we read to each other. When we turned off the light, we laid on opposite sides of my queen-sized bed like stick figures. If I hadn't broken my neck, we might have cuddled, might even have had sex, but if I hadn't broken my neck he wouldn't have been there.

Ten months after the accident he hadn't left. We went back to my summer cottage. The bay and swimming in it, the antidote to the fire thirty-seven years before, was still the place I felt peaceful and restored. However it was impossible to turn my head very far anymore because of my fused spine. Bruce stayed close in the water so I didn't drown as I tried different ways to swim a fraction of my past daily one-thousand strokes. Instead of the crawl, I floated on my back, chin tucked, facing the cerulean sky bicycling my legs, arms swooshing overhead. It didn't take me the distance, but looking up at the sky and moving through the water made me feel radiant and still conjured the optimism and grand ideas that came to me while buoyant.

Who knows what the world or my life will be like in the future. I continue to be the reed once a shoot, now tall and deeply rooted but still pliant, swayed by the wind.

ACKNOWLEDGMENTS

Jaime, aka Reign, my son, who demonstrates and has taught me endless love, acceptance and patience;

Bruce, my rock, who has given family a widened definition. His love and encouragement is a constant and provides a solid ground where I can take flight and land;

Xeni Fragakis, Nick Flynn, Mark Matousek, Daphne Merkin, and Susan Shapiro who have helped me to become a better writer of memoir;

Scott Edward Anderson for his generosity as a writer and friend;

Jonathan Santiofer for his encouragement and advice;

Jill Rothenberg for her editorial insight;

Nancy Austin for her emotional support;

Phyllis Hott for her deep friendship and encouragement;

Anam Cara, where in the isolation of Ireland's Beara peninsula, I had time to think and put my story in the first person on its way to becoming a memoir; and

Christine Cote for her enthusiasm, flexibility, and patience as a publisher and editor.

ABOUT THE AUTHOR

Photo: Susan Rosenberg Jones

BRAHNA YASSKY came to the written word through her paintings when she started writing stories about the images she created. *Slow Dancing with Fire* is her debut book. Her essays have been published in *The Plentitudes Journal, American Writers Review 2020, Wired, The Independent, Salon,* AARP's *The Ethel*, among others. Trained as a visual artist at California College of the Arts and San Francisco State University, her work has been exhibited widely, including at The San Francisco Museum of Modern Art, The Jersey City Museum, The Hudson River Museum, The Bali Purnati Center. She also received commissions from the New York City Department of Health for public art projects. She lives in Brooklyn, New York, and East Hampton, New York.

www.brahnayassky.com
Facebook @brahnayassky
Instagram @brahnayassky